Duncaster

D1378426

America Pictured to the Life

ILLUSTRATED WORKS
from THE PAUL MELLON BEQUEST

By
George A. Miles and William S. Reese

The Beinecke Rare Book & Manuscript Library
Yale University
Distributed by
University Press of New England

This book accompanies the exhibition
America Pictured to the Life: Illustrated Works from the Paul Mellon Bequest
held at the Beinecke Rare Book & Manuscript Library,
Yale University, New Haven, Connecticut
from May 3 through July 31, 2002.

ILLUSTRATIONS:

JACKET FRONT
Bollings Dam, Petersburgh, Virginia from Joshua Shaw and John Hill,
PICTURESQUE VIEWS OF AMERICAN SCENERY,
Philadelphia, 1820. Hand-colored aquatint. (catalog entry 5)

JACKET BACK
A battle between Eskimos and Vikings from Heinrich Rink, editor,
KALADLIT OKALLUKTUALLIAIT,
Godthaab, 1859-1863. Hand-colored woodcut. (catalog entry 32)

FRONTISPIECE
Summer. No. 3. A Road Accident; a glimpse thro' an opening of the Primitive Forest, Thornville, Ohio
from George Harvey, *HARVEY'S SCENES OF THE PRIMITIVE FOREST OF AMERICA*,
New York (but actually London), 1841.
Hand colored lithograph. (catalog entry 7)

HALF TITLE
Sigismund Bacstrom, *Tchua, a Chief of Queen Charlotte's Island in Lat 52″ 12′ N*, 1793.
Pen, ink and watercolor. (catalog entry 43)

PAGE 125
Sigismund Bacstrom, *A Chief at Nootka, sitting on the ground*, ca. 1793.
Pen, ink, and watercolor. (catalog entry 43)

Library of Congress Cataloging-in-Publication Data

Beinecke Rare Book and Manuscript Library.
America pictured to the life : illustrated works from the Paul Mellon bequest /
by George A. Miles and William S. Reese.
p. cm.
This book accompanies the exhibition *America Pictured to the Life: Illustrated Works from the Paul Mellon Bequest* held at the Beinecke Rare
Book & Manuscript Library, Yale University, New Haven, Connecticut
from May 3 through July 31, 2002.
Includes index.
ISBN 0-8457-3138-6 (alk. paper)
1. America—Civilization—Sources—Bibliography—Exhibitions.
2. America—Early works to 1800—Exhibitions.
3. America—Maps—Exhibitions. 4. Illustrated books—Connecticut—
New Haven—Exhibitions. 5. Rare books—Connecticut—New Haven—Exhibitions.
6. Beinecke Rare Book and Manuscript Library—Exhibitions.
I. Miles, George A. II. Reese, William S. III. Title.
Z1201 .B46 2002
[E20]
016.97—dc21

PRINTED IN SINGAPORE

Foreword

As proud as the Beinecke Library's staff is of our collections, we were humbled by the splendor of Paul Mellon's bequest. From manuscripts and printed works documenting early European exploration of the Americas, to accounts of French participation in the American Revolution, to dozens of rare color plate books, and major accounts of Native American life, the gift reflects the quality, the range, and the depth of Mr. Mellon's Americana collection. We stand in awe and gratitude.

The gift strengthens the opportunities for scholars and students to explore American history and culture at the Beinecke Library. As a spectacular example, Henri Crublier d'Opterre's manuscript account of the French army's march from Newport to Yorktown and Louis Antoine de Bouganville's journals of French naval operations during the Revolution join the Rochambeau papers (which Mr. Mellon gave to the library in 1992), the Benjamin Franklin collection, and papers of Alexis de Tocqueville and Gustave de Beaumont to make Yale not only a premier repository at which to examine the military and diplomatic history of the American Revolution but also an extraordinary place at which to explore French-American cultural interaction throughout the early national period.

Mr. Mellon's Native American collections have already provided new opportunities for two scholars engaged in major research projects. For a graduate student at Yale in American Studies who is writing a dissertation on Sir William Johnson, the unpublished letters and journals of Guy Johnson, Sir William's nephew and assistant, have been invaluable. For a curator from the Joslyn Museum who is undertaking the first thorough investigation of the publishing history of Maximilian of Wied's account of his trip to the American West, Mr. Mellon's copy of the German edition in uncut, unfolded sheets with uncolored plates will be essential.

The value of the Mellon gift lies not only in famous and unique items, but also in the many lesser-known works that enhance Beinecke's collections in fields we have long pursued. The series of children's books published by McLoughlin Brothers adds wonderfully to our strong collection of American children's literature. The numerous early-national imprints about American architecture, carpentry, and drawing offer fabulous insights into the life of artisans as well as the history of American trade publishing. The many illustrated accounts of travel to Latin America strengthen an area of collecting in which Yale faculty and students have expressed renewed interest in recent years.

This catalog and the exhibition it records can include only a fraction of Paul Mellon's Americana collection, but we are confident that it bears witness to his intellectual curiosity, his sagacity as a collector, and his generosity as a benefactor. As the benficiaries of his trust, we look forward to sharing his wisdom with students and scholars from around the world.

Barbara A. Shailor
Director, Beinecke Rare Book & Manuscript Library

Introduction

Paul Mellon will probably be best remembered as an art collector and a benefactor of museums. He was also one of the greatest book collectors of the twentieth century, and, either personally or through the foundations to which he gave life and direction, the greatest supporter of research libraries the United States has known. His gifts to libraries, by their nature, are not as visible to the public eye as his donations of institutions like the National Gallery of Art or the Yale Center for British Art. Their importance is every bit as great. This catalog attempts to illustrate some of the riches within one small part of the many Mellon gifts and bequests to Yale and to libraries throughout the nation.

Yale's greatest donor, Mr. Mellon was an extraordinarily generous friend to the libraries of the University throughout his life. From shortly after his graduation, he contributed a broad range of treasures that have immeasurably enhanced the research opportunities of readers at the Yale Center for British Art, Sterling Memorial Library, and the Beinecke Rare Book and Manuscript Library. These gifts demonstrate how far-ranging his bookish interests were. Virtually the entire rare book collection at the Center for British Art was contributed by Mellon, while the Beinecke and other Yale libraries were given, or received assistance in purchasing, materials as disparate as the Boswell Papers and Mr. Mellon's marvelous assemblage of books and manuscripts on alchemy and the occult.

After Mellon's death the Yale collections were the primary beneficiary of the distribution of his remaining books. The bulk of these – some 7500 items – were left to the Center for British Art. Among these was his collection of sporting books, a theme he pursued from his student days at Clare College, Cambridge, until his death. The Center also received his modern English fine printing collection, as well as those atlases, maps, and illustrated topographical works that had not already been turned over during his life. Finally, the Center and the Beinecke Library received a substantial part of his collection of printed and manuscript Americana, which was divided among Yale, the University of Virginia, and the Virginia Historical Society. The material in this exhibition is drawn from the Americana portion of the bequest.

If Mellon's patronage of books and libraries was far less visible than his activities in the arts, the Americana segment of his book collection was the most hidden of all. With a few notable exceptions such as the Rochambeau papers, given to the Beinecke in 1992, he retained almost all of the materials during his lifetime, largely housed in the Old Library at the Brick House on his estate in Upperville, Virginia. Unlike his sporting books, the Abbey collection of illustrated topographical works, or his alchemy collection, there was no published catalog. Nor was it ever publicly exhibited, as was his collection of William Blake or his early English books. The Americana, though linked in many ways to his other collections, remained a private enthusiasm.

An early turning point in Mellon's book collecting was his acquisition, between 1953 and 1956, of the vast collection of illustrated books on topography, travel, and the arts formed by Major John R. Abbey. Abbey took as his theme the heyday of the English illustrated book, in the mediums of aquatint and lithography, between 1770 and 1860. He compiled three superb catalogs of his collection which remain standard references in the field: *Scenery of Great Britain and Ireland in Aquatint and Lithography* (1952), *Life in England in Aquatint and Lithography* (1953), and *Travel in Aquatint and Lithography* (1956). Mellon bought the books and portfolios described in the English catalogs in 1953, adding the travel books when Abbey had completed the final volume. The Abbey collection was kept almost entirely intact, and was turned over to the Center for British Art in stages from 1977 until the final bequest.

The travel section of the Abbey collection contained about a hundred titles relating to the Americas, of which only twenty-two were about the United States, the weakest section. Of course, all of the other genres Abbey had collected, such as works on architecture, books on drawing and art instruction, panoramas, what used to be generally classified as "sports and pastimes," and scenes of local topography, were confined to Great Britain, with a few Continental exceptions. Looking at the magnificent collection he had acquired, Mellon decided to continue to build it, adding works which fit the Abbey criteria but had eluded the Major.

In 1957 and 1958, Mellon evidently resolved to build an American version of the Abbey collection, and it was this decision which informed much of his collecting of Americana. Starting with the large view books, and later spreading his net to include many genres beyond Abbey's criteria, he built a library of books, portfolios, pamphlets, cartography, and manuscripts whose unifying theme was illustration. The Americana also expanded beyond Abbey's time window, ultimately ranging from the first illustrated Americanum, a 1494 account of Columbus' first voyage, to items from the early twentieth century. What began as "American Abbey" grew into a much more comprehensive assemblage of visual source material for American history, life, and culture.

Mellon was active as a collector of Americana books and manuscripts for about fifteen years, until the early 1970s. By then, his determination to build the English collections that founded the Center for British Art pushed his American interests aside. Although he acquired notable books and manuscripts within the genre before and after those dates, it was during that decade and a half that he purchased several thousand separate items, often of staggering rarity, making his one of the finest collections ever formed in the field. The majority of his acquisitions concerned two distinct themes: material relating to the history of his adopted home state of Virginia, or illustrated works relating to American history in the broadest sense. Mellon was keenly interested in providing research materials within Virginia's borders, and in the dispersal of the collection most of the Virginiana went to the University of Virginia or the Virginia Historical Society. Although Yale received some magnificent Virginia books already held by the University and the Historical Society, the bulk of the nearly 800 items that it received from Mr. Mellon's estate came from the general Americana segment of his collection.

Limited to ninety-eight entries, the present catalog and the Beinecke Library exhibit that it records represent only a small fraction of Paul Mellon's final bequest to Yale's libraries. Among the items omitted are many of great beauty and extraordinary rarity. They include, for example, the German edition of Prince Maximilian of Wied-Neuwied's *Reise in das innere Nord-Amerika* (Coblenz, 1839), in which the hand-colored engravings after Carl Bodmer's watercolors are present in unbound parts, as issued, each part in its original paper wrappers. Significant manuscripts, including the papers of Guy Johnson, secretary to the British Superintendent of Indian Affairs during and after the French and Indian Wars, and the lengthy folio ledger entitled *The Accompts of Her Majesties Revenues in America* from the papers of British crown officer William Blathwayt are also unrepresented. Space and our chosen themes have limited what we can show.

Despite the necessary omissions, the items described here are broadly representative of Mr. Mellon's diverse interests in American history and culture. Among the earliest works are Theodor de Bry's 1594 illustrated German translation of Girolamo Benzoni's account of his travels in the new world and a rare 1622 edition of Giovanni Botero's economic geography of the world, *Le Relationi Universali*, featuring woodcuts of fantastic creatures who reputedly lived beyond Europe's borders. Four centuries removed from the reports of Europe's first encounters with America are works that reflect both the revolution in printing technology that occurred in the nineteenth century and the cultural transformations that accompanied European expansion. *Buffalo Bill's Wild West Panorama for Children* (ca. 1890) and *The Brownie Blocks* (1891) employ chromolithography to create dramatic illustrations for children's amusement and education. Between these chronological extremes appear works from Europe and the Americas representing virtually every major form of illustration and a wide variety of literary genres.

The catalog and exhibit are intended not only to explore the character of Mellon's collecting interests, but also to suggest to scholars and students some of the many opportunities for research made possible by the bequest. To this end, the organization of the material departs from conventional approaches to illustrated books and manuscripts. Much of the bibliographic and scholarly discussion of such works has focused upon the techniques of illustration (for example, woodcuts, aquatints, or lithographs), the careers of important artists, craftsmen, and publishers (such as George Catlin, Julius Bien, or Currier & Ives), or a specific genre (children's literature or costume books). These studies provide great insight into the mechanics of illustration and the role that leading figures played in the trade, but they tend to focus our attention upon the physical characteristics of particular types or genres of illustration. Rarely do they consider the ways that assembled illustrations function as visual texts with their own distinctive rhetoric and vocabulary. The arrangement of the catalog and the discussion of individual works are intended to explore that language and to draw attention to some of the ways in which illustrated works may serve as primary evidence of the social and cultural forces that created and consumed them.

As interesting and useful as a single print or drawing can be in depicting a lost scene or historical moment, the meaning and significance of illustrations in books, portfolios, and manuscripts often lies less in the content of any individual picture than in the relationship of the images to each other and to the written text itself. We hope that the four categories by which we have arranged the catalog, *Visual Directories*, *History*, *Utility*, and *Arts & Amusements*, suggest some of the kinds of "conversations" that occur within and among illustrated works. The categories emerged from our examination and handling of the Mellon bequest rather than from any preconceived scheme. We recognize that unlike such technical terms as *relief* or *intaglio*, our categories are not mutually exclusive. We regard them not as a rigid system of classification but as a means to encourage the imaginative consideration of particular titles and illustrated work in general.

By *Visual Directories* we mean illustrated topographical works, either portfolios of prints or plates combined with written commentary, that depict not only the landscape, but also cultural life and built environment of a place. Akin to city directories, which provided a list of the residents, professions, and businesses of a particular town at a particular time, visual directories offered a virtual tour of the scenes and views that readers might have expected to see during a visit. Characteristically, they reflect a particular time as well as a specific place.

History includes works meant to depict the events or personalities that had shaped the world of the illustrator and his intended audience. They may be imaginary or documentary, derived from legends or from immediate experience. Their scale ranges from epic depictions of warfare to personal recollections of private life. Like written histories, such works may distort the past as they seek to shape how it is understood by author and reader alike.

Utility consists of practical illustration, from technical manuals to scientific explanation to various forms of advertisement. It is undoubtedly anachronistic to describe such illustration as commercial art, but it is reasonable to see in it the harbinger of later developments. Whether depicting banister designs, geologic strata, California grapes, or the process of chromolithography itself, these works place great emphasis upon the fidelity of their reproductions. Where the works of *Arts & Amusements* often sought to stir the emotions, works of *Utility* offered a convenient, portable alternative to the examination of products and natural phenomena.

Within our final category, *Arts & Amusements*, we include works meant to edify and entertain or to teach the fine arts. From drawing manuals to satirical narratives of college life, from sheet music to religious and children's literature, illustration contributed to the lesson or sharpened the moral. Although the illustrations in such works sometimes share in the specificity of place and time characteristic of *Visual Directories* and works of *History*, they more often serve as general types, meant to illustrate skills, attitudes, and values rather than particular people or places.

If asked to place this catalog within our categories, we would probably argue that it is all of the above: a utilitarian description that provides a visual directory of Paul Mellon's bequest, which we hope illuminates the history of illustration in an entertaining fashion. To the extent that it is any of these, it reflects the breadth and depth of Paul Mellon's collection. We offer this catalog as a small token of our gratitude for the generous gift that he and his executors have presented to the libraries of Yale University.

Visual Directories

Illustrated topographical works, either portfolios of prints or plates combined with written commentary, provide a visual text describing not only the landscape, but also cultural life and the constructed environment. Although there are numerous individual prints and illustrations from earlier dates, the first major work to depict a sequence of places in North America and the Caribbean is the *Scenographia Americana*, published in London in the 1760s. William Birch's views of Philadelphia, published there in 1800, were the first such produced in the Western Hemisphere. Virtually all of the major view books of North America were issued in the early to mid-nineteenth century, and executed in the dominant media of the day: aquatint, lithography, and chromolithography.

Compared to the rich European tradition of topographical works and illustrated travel books, the genre never reached its full potential in North America and the United States. Of the works produced, many were actually manufactured in London, Paris, or Germany. All were heavily dependent on European expatriate artists and printers. These craftsmen drew on their continental training and tastes as they created views of their adopted homeland. The comparatively high cost and narrow market for color plate books doomed many of the projects to small circulation or, if they were issued by subscription over time as was typical, to premature demise. The lack of a wealthy audience probably accounts both for the paucity of such works and their rarity today.

The books and prints shown here range in point of view from the literal to the romantic. As with any text, the motive of the author or artist has to be considered when reading them. At one extreme, Shaw and Hill, in creating their *Picturesque Views*, were frankly imbued with the popular theories of Burke and Gilpin on the sublime and the picturesque. On the other hand, urban boosters such as Whelpley and Onken created literal representations of Cleveland and Cincinnati which froze moments in the development of those cities. Some, such as Carl Nebel in Mexico, attempted to give an overview of the culture and life of a country, while others, such as the British diplomat Anthony St. John Baker, provided an intensely personal view of one individual's travels. All give the modern viewer a fresh way of seeing the life and landscape of America.

1

Thomas Pownall

SIX REMARKABLE VIEWS IN THE PROVINCES OF NEW YORK, NEW JERSEY AND PENNSYLVANIA

London, 1761

The first great series of plates to depict the English colonies in North America was the *Scenographia Americana.* The twenty-eight mezzotints which make up a complete set, illustrating scenes from Canada to the West Indies at the time of the Seven Years' War, were originally issued in separate fascicles by different artists between 1760 and 1763, then combined as a single work in 1768. The *Six Remarkable Views* were based on drawings by the prominent colonial administrator Thomas Pownall. These mezzotints were not originally intended to be colored, but were meant to achieve their effect through subtle contrast of light and shade. When sets were colored, as here, a thick, rich application of paints sought to imitate the look of original artwork.

1. *A View of the Great Cohoes Falls, on the Mohawk River.* Hand-colored mezzotint.

2. No. 3 (Untitled view of a home and its well). Aquatint.

2

Abner Reed

VIEWS OF CONNECTICUT

Hartford, 1809

A native of East Windsor, Connecticut, Reed was a self-taught engraver whose illustrations appeared as early as 1793. He also wrote the first novel by a Connecticut author, *Love Triumphant*, in 1797. Reed built a varied business in Hartford, working on everything from bank notes to encyclopedia illustrations, although the great mass of his work was ephemeral in nature. In 1809, experimenting in aquatint, he produced this modest series of views taken from scenes around Hartford. They reflect a purely American strain of workmanship, based on Yankee improvisation rather than European schooling.

3. *Back of the State House, Philadelphia.* Hand-colored engraving.

3

William Russell Birch

THE CITY OF PHILADELPHIA, IN THE STATE OF PENNSYLVANIA NORTH AMERICA; AS IT APPEARED IN THE YEAR 1800

Springland Cottage, Pennsylvania, 1800

Birch's series of engravings of Philadelphia, then the largest city in the United States, was the first work to record both the buildings and people of urban America in any detail. Rather than exhibiting a static iconography of the most notable architecture, Birch produced a series of street scenes which draw the viewer into the life of the town. Each plate is a moment frozen in time, a snapshot that shows the inhabitants strolling, conversing, or working in their everyday lives, with different street corners or prominent buildings as their backdrop. The artist succeeded in giving the viewer an intimate sense of the life of the city as well as its chief monuments.

4. *No. 1. – Birds-eye view taken from Mr. Catlin's model which was made from a careful survey.* Hand-colored lithograph.

4

George Catlin

VIEWS OF NIAGARA, DRAWN ON STONE AND COLORED FROM NATURE

New York, 1831

Famous for his watercolor portraits of western Native Americans, George Catlin began his artistic career in upstate New York. His first published illustration was of the construction of the Erie Canal at Lockport, which appeared in Cadwallader Colden's 1825 report about the Canal to the City Council of New York. Later he joined William Dunlap, Asher Durand, and John Casilear to propose publishing by subscription an illustrated history of the city of New York and its environs "from the earliest settlement, to the establishment of the federal government." This volume of eight color plates represents Catlin's first separate publication. Like most of Catlin's work, it enjoyed little commercial success during his lifetime. It is one of only three copies known to have survived.

5. *View by Moonlight, near Fayetteville.*
Hand-colored aquatint.

5

Joshua Shaw and John Hill

PICTURESQUE VIEWS OF AMERICAN SCENERY

Painted by J. Shaw. Engraved by J. Hill.
Philadelphia, 1820

Known as "The Landscape Album," this portfolio of views was a collaboration between the artist Joshua Shaw and the aquatint engraver John Hill. Although both men had only recently arrived from England when they undertook the work, Shaw felt sufficiently Americanized to speak in the first person when he wrote: "Our country abounds with Scenery, comprehending all the varieties of the sublime, the beautiful, and the picturesque in nature, worthy to engage the skill of an Artist. . . ." Each plate seeks to convey the unique spirit of place of disparate locations throughout the United States. Although the scenery was American, the romantic sensibility behind it was indicative of the European background and training of its creators.

6. *View Near Norwich, Ct.* Tinted lithograph.

6
Edwin Whitefield
AMERICAN VIEWS
New York, 1847

Whitefield was a jack-of-all-trades, supporting himself as a traveling artist by commissioned paintings of estates, giving art lessons, and selling artists' supplies and a series of published views and art instruction manuals. His peripatetic life allowed him to gather materials for several series of American views, of which this volume is the first. He was also skilled enough as a lithographer to execute his drawings on stone; this series was self-published in New York, and mainly reflects his work in the Hudson Valley. Yet another emigrant, Whitefield was born in England and came to the United States via Canada, where he also traveled and worked extensively.

7
George Harvey
HARVEY'S SCENES OF THE PRIMITIVE FOREST OF AMERICA . . .
New York (but actually London), 1841

Harvey, an English artist who resided in the United States for many years, was intrigued by what he felt to be the unique nature of American light. He proposed publishing a portfolio of forty lithographs depicting "Atmospheric Landscapes." Four of these were to show "Epochs of the Year," while the other thirty-six would illustrate points in the day from misty dawn to moonlit midnight, or "Different Epochs of the Day." Each scene would be set in a different geographical locale in the United States. Sadly, only the first part of this wonderful project, that showing the seasons, was published as the present work. The luminous hand-colored lithographs fulfill Harvey's vision of the distinctive slant of light in the American forests.

7. *Spring. No. 2. Burning Fallen Trees in a Girdled Clearing. Western Scene.* Hand-colored lithograph.

8

Anthony St. John Baker

MEMOIRES D'UN VOYAGEUR QUI SE REPOSE

London, 1850

The author was a British diplomat who spent many years in the United States. After his retirement he assembled the diaries of his various travels, mainly in America, and had them privately printed, evidently for circulation among his family. Only three sets were produced. Baker illustrated two of them with original watercolors and drawings he had made on the spot in his excursions, mainly summer trips from Washington D.C. northward to New York, New England, and Canada. These constitute a wonderful collection of views of towns and places in the United States from 1811 to 1832, as seen by an astute observer who was sometimes accused of being a spy as well.

9

Augustus Kollner

VIEWS OF THE MOST INTERESTING OBJECTS AND SCENERY IN THE UNITED STATES OF AMERICA

New York (but actually Paris), 1848–1851

German by birth, Kollner trained as an engraver and lithographer in Paris before emigrating to the United States in 1839. He traveled extensively as a portrait painter and creator of views before establishing himself in Philadelphia, where he was a fixture of the artistic community until his death in 1906. His superb views of Baltimore, Philadelphia, New York, and other American cities were not entrusted to American lithographers but sent to Paris, where they could be produced to a higher standard than would have been possible in the United States. There are numerous instances in the nineteenth century of artists working in America sending their work to Europe to be engraved or lithographed. Sometimes these imported plates were given false imprints to suggest that they were produced locally.

8. *New Haven, Ct. from the West Mountain.* Pen, ink, and wash drawing.

9. *Broad-way.*
Hand-colored lithograph.

10. *View on the Ohio River below Cincinnati.* Lithograph.

10

G. N. Frankenstein

THE WESTERN PORT FOLIO. CONTAINING SKETCHES OF WESTERN SCENERY

Cincinnati, 1840

The four prints in this modest and virtually unknown portfolio are among the earliest lithographs to be produced in Cincinnati. Their creator was one of six artistic siblings, raised in Germany, who emigrated to Ohio in 1831. All had careers as artists, but Godfrey was by far the most successful, progressing from sign painter's apprentice to first president of the Cincinnati Academy of Fine Arts in 1841. The printed wrapper which accompanies the prints styles them "Vol. 1," suggesting this is another instance in which a proposed larger project, conceived by entrepreneurship and civic pride, died for lack of subscribers. Frankenstein went on to create a panorama of Niagara Falls which was widely exhibited in the 1850s.

11. *Cleveland, Ohio. From the Courthouse Looking West.* Hand-colored lithograph.

11

Thomas Whelpley

FOUR VIEWS OF CLEVELAND

New York, 1833

Whelpley's depiction of Cleveland reflects his background as a surveyor. The opening of the Ohio Canal in 1827, following the completion of the Erie Canal in 1825, made the lakeshore town the nexus of commerce between the Ohio back country and the East, heralding an era of explosive growth and development. Whelpley produced a strictly linear view of the city, emphasizing careful depiction of the many new buildings, most of which were less than a decade old.

12. *Main Street, Between Fourth and Fifth.* Hand-colored lithograph.

12
Otto Onken
VIEWS OF CINCINNATI
Cincinnati, ca. 1850

Cincinnati became the first major center of publishing west of the Alleghenies. A large community of lithographers, mostly German emigrants, was established there by 1847, when Otto Onken opened his press. He probably published this series of street scenes about 1850, showing in exact detail the main commercial thoroughfares of the town. Such images both advertised the merchants in the view and appealed to the civic spirit of the rapidly expanding metropolis. "The reader will forgive a little natural pride," Onken states the next year in his viewbook, *Western Scenery*, "For who would not be proud of the 'Queen City of the West'?"

13. *Baton Rouge, Louisiana.* Chromolithograph.

13
Henry Lewis
DAS ILLUSTRIRTE MISSISSIPPITHAL . . .

Düsseldorf, 1858

Lewis conceived the idea of painting a panorama of the entire Mississippi River, a project which took him three years. The finished work was in two sections, each twelve feet high by a quarter mile long. It was displayed in theatres on rollers, taking the viewer from the headwaters of the river in Minnesota to New Orleans. Lewis toured the panorama around the United States and Europe after its completion in 1849. This color plate book grew out of the larger project, and was published in Germany, where Lewis had settled. It is the closest surviving remnant we have to the several epic panoramas of the Mississippi created in the mid-nineteenth century, all of which are now lost.

14

John Caspar Wild

THE VALLEY OF THE MISSISSIPPI ILLUSTRATED IN A SERIES OF VIEWS

St. Louis, 1841–1842

This is the first illustrated book printed west of the Mississippi. Once again, European training underlay an American product. The artist John Caspar Wild, originally from Zurich, emigrated to Philadelphia in the early 1830s. There he published *Views Of Philadelphia . . .*, which established a formula used again in this work: a series of individual scenes around the city, capped off with a four-part panorama. In St. Louis, Wild executed his sweeping vista of the city from the roof of the Planter's Hotel. As with so many books issued in parts, the final numbers are far rarer than the first, and the Yale Western Americana Collection has for decades sought a complete set of this book. The superb Mellon copy is in the original printed wrappers.

14. *North.* From a panorama of St. Louis. Lithograph.

15. *St. Ann's: The Governor's Residence.* Lithograph.

15

Richard Bridgens

WEST INDIA SCENERY, WITH ILLUSTRATIONS OF NEGRO CHARACTER . . .

London, 1836

Bridgens, a British architect whose wife had inherited a sugar plantation, lived in Trinidad for seven years at the end of the era of slavery in the British West Indian colonies. The sugar industry, long a source of extraordinary wealth for Europeans, went into decline in the nineteenth century as cheaper sweeteners undercut the market, and economic and moral imperatives combined to bring the gradual emancipation of slaves after 1833. The plates in this work reflect these changes; scenes from the everyday lives of slaves are shown with comparative sensitivity, but slave punishments are also depicted. In the topographical scenes, the specialized landscape of the elaborate infrastructure of sugar production is central.

16. *Vista del Fondo de la Bahia de la Habana.* Tinted lithograph.

16

D. Federico Mialhe

VIAGE PINTORESCO AL REDEDOR DE LA ISLA DE CUBA

Havana, 1848

Important illustrated works were produced in Latin America as well as the United States. Havana in the early nineteenth century was a city of extraordinary wealth and culture. Although a Spanish colony, the elite of Cuba looked entirely to France for their luxuries. One aspect of this Francophile sophistication was a talented community of lithographers made up almost entirely of emigrant Parisian workmen. Mialhe, perhaps the foremost of these, produced a series of viewbooks of the island in a variety of formats after he moved there in 1836.

17

G. W. C. Voorduin

GEZIGTEN VIT NEERLAND'S WEST-INDIEN, NAAR DE NATUUR GETEEKEND

Amsterdam, ca. 1859

Voorduin was a Dutch naval officer who visited many of the Dutch colonial possessions in South America and the West Indies in the 1850s. Included are numerous scenes in Surinam, a series of views on the island of Curaçao, and plates of Bonaire, St. Eustatius, St. Martin, and Saba. In Surinam he depicted a plantation society still dependent on slavery; the former sugar islands of the Caribbean were largely sunken in somnolence. The plates were beautifully printed in chromolithography by the Amsterdam firm of Franz Buffa.

17. *Suriname: Een Plantaadge Slavenkamp.*
Hand-colored lithograph.

18.
Casa del Emperador Iturbide.
Hand-colored lithograph.

19. *Plaza Mayor de Guadalajara*. Hand-colored lithograph.

18

MEXICO Y SUS ALREDEDORES

Mexico, 1864

Within Mexico, a lively homegrown lithographic industry began in 1826, and found broad expression in primarily black and white images. This book, which went through a complicated evolution of editions from 1856 to 1869 that vary widely in content, is the single most important color plate book produced in Mexico in the age of lithography. It depicts scenes in and around the City of Mexico during an era of development, civil war, and foreign invasion; which party controlled the capitol influenced the addition and subtraction of some plates from successive editions.

19

Carl Nebel

VOYAGE PITTORESQUE ET ARCHÉOLOGIQUE DANS LA PARTIE LA PLUS INTÉRESSANTE DU MEXIQUE

Paris, 1836

The artist, a Prussian architect, traveled extensively in Mexico. He was drawn there at first by an interest in the archeological remnants of the Aztec empire, but became a visual chronicler of modern Mexico as well. Nebel was one of many European artists intrigued by the landscape and peoples of the former Spanish empire in the Americas, barred from view for centuries, but from the 1820s onward open to both travel and investment, and of particular interest to the French and English. His book combines a taste for the picturesque with a clear-eyed evaluation of the country and its assets.

20. Scenes from the *Central Park Album*. Chromolithographs.

20

CENTRAL PARK ALBUM

Boston, 1864

This charming little accordion-fold album of twelve plates was printed by Louis Prang of Boston, already launched on his career as the most important chromolithographer in the United States. Central Park had been laid out and largely completed under the direction of Frederick Law Olmsted and Calvert Vaux between early 1859 and the summer of 1861. Although its completion had been delayed by the Civil War, it was already a notable New York sight, as this souvenir viewbook testifies. The individual chromolithographs show landmarks, mainly architectural, in the Park.

21

Edward Vischer

VISCHER'S VIEWS OF CALIFORNIA. THE MAMMOTH TREE GROVE AND ITS AVENUES. CALAVERAS COUNTY, CALIFORNIA

San Francisco, 1862

After a varied life as a merchant in Latin America and the Orient, Vischer settled in California during the gold rush. He originally took up drawing for amusement, gradually turning his art into a full-time business in the 1860s. His books illustrate the mining regions and the Yosemite area, primarily with photographs of Vischer's original

21. (Above) Illustrated title page.
Tinted lithograph.
(Right) *Log of the Original Big Tree, 1855.* Albumen photograph.

drawings and paintings. There are no contemporary publications quite comparable to them in their eccentric combination of media; the confusion is compounded by the bewildering array of formats, issues, and reissues the artist ultimately produced. The Mellon bequest contains two issues of this work, quite different in their internal makeup.

22

Paul Emmert

SIX VIEWS OF HONOLULU

San Francisco, 1854

This impressive series of six large folio lithographs gives a comprehensive record of the city of Honolulu in the early 1850s. Each plate has a large central view, surrounded by numerous vignettes of specific business establishments and homes, for a total of one hundred separate images of the town. Emmert, a Swiss artist who had established an engraving and lithographic studio in Honolulu, was certainly not equipped to produce any plates on this scale, and the lithographs were published by the leading San Francisco firm of Britton & Rey, who had issued many similar views of gold rush towns in California. Such town views were a staple of American print publishing from the 1850s onward.

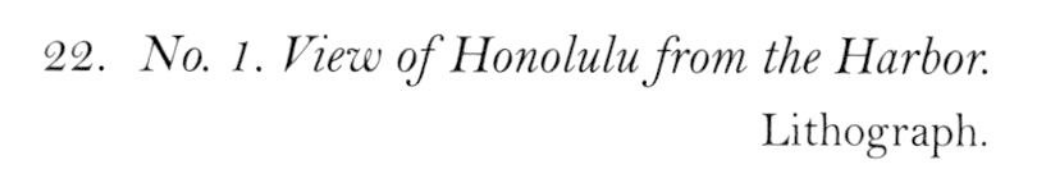
22. *No. 1. View of Honolulu from the Harbor.*
Lithograph.

INTERIOR OF THE FORT.
MARKET HOUSE.
CHARITY SCHOOL
STONE CHURCH.
BETHEL.
SWAN & CLIFFORD
PALACE OF KING KAMEHAMEHA III.
COURT HOUSE.
ARMORY.
Lith. of Britton & Rey.
Published by Paul Emmert.
Sketched from nature by Paul Emmert.
No. 1.
VIEW OF HONOLULU.

23. *Great Fire on Lake Street.* Hand-colored lithograph.

23

CHICAGO ILLUSTRATED

Chicago, 1866–1867

This superb series of fifty-two views of Chicago in 1866 is the most complete visual record available of the city before the Great Fire of 1871. The plates were executed by the local firm of Jevne and Almini and were issued in both tinted and colored state. The work portrays the surging, bustling growth of the city after the Civil War, illustrating different street corners, the view from various bridges over the Chicago River, key public buildings and hotels, and local wonders such as the Stock Yards and the Water Works. *Chicago Illustrated* captured the spirit of an American city of the Gilded Age as Birch had captured that of Philadelphia in 1800.

History

Illustrated works of American history trace their origins to the sixteenth century. As Europeans recognized that Columbus had found a new world rather than a new route to the Indies, they became increasingly conscious that voyages of exploration and encounters with the people and resources of America were transforming their own world in unprecedented ways. Words alone could not express the wonder, awe, and fascination inspired by news from foreign lands. Pictures, some based on an artist's immediate experience, others on little more than imagination, not only supplemented written texts but often conveyed their own narrative.

The decades-long project of Theodor de Bry and his sons to publish a multi-volume set documenting the grand voyages to America exemplifies the complicated, inconsistent, and confusing effort of Europeans to represent the story of their initial contact with America. For the first volume in the series, published in 1591, de Bry worked closely with an eyewitness artist, John White, to illustrate Thomas Hariot's account of the English colony at Roanoke. For his second volume, de Bry relied upon drawings by Jacques Le Moyne reconstructing his experiences in America, but de Bry had no communication with the artist to resolve questions about the scenes or their details. From the fourth volume to the end of the project, virtually all the illustrations were the work of artists in Europe who provided their own interpretive gloss upon the texts.

The multiple sources and story lines that developed within de Bry's volumes reflect the tensions that appear in many illustrated histories. Pictures could be used to reinforce or to diminish the themes of the written text. Like words, they could be more or less accurate representations of the events they described, meant to reveal or to obscure. Whether "true" or "false," they have proven useful evidence for contemporary scholars attempting to understand better the values, interests, and attitudes of their makers as well as the nature of public discourse about the past, present, and future prospects of America. As we read them today we can hear echoes of earlier conversations.

Most of the works described below share the epic scale of de Bry: world geographies, tales of war, accounts of circumnavigation and political upheaval. These grand events dominated all historical writing until recent decades so it is not surprising to find them heavily represented here. What may surprise, however, is how many of these works contain within them an intensely personal view of the larger events: the autobiography of an Icelandic Inuit visiting Copenhagen, anonymous sketches of unidentified French-Canadian fur trappers, and the story of an enlisted man serving in the Union Army during the Civil War remind us that history happens, and is interpreted, on many scales.

24
Giovanni Botero
LE RELATIONI UNIVERSALI DI GIOVANNI BOTERO BENESE . . .

Venice, 1622–1623

Originally published in Rome in 1591, Botero's work is often described as an early attempt to define the world economy. In 1618 and 1622, the Venetian printer and sometime author Alessandro de Vecchi reprinted Botero's work, adding to it his own thirty-two-leaf appendix, "Aggiunta alla quarta parte dell'Indie... Di monstri, & Usanze di quelle parti, di quei re con le sue figure al naturale." Vecchi's text is illustrated with full-page woodcuts, including fifteen monsters that may have been based on Pliny and other fabulist authors, but here purport to represent the kinds of creatures found outside Europe. Other woodcuts, depicting natives of India, Africa, and Arabia, were printed from pieces of a large block cut by Hans Burgkmair to illustrate an early sixteenth-century narrative of a voyage to Southern India.

24. Untitled woodcut.

Columbus als er in India erstlich ankommen/wirdt von den Einwohnern mit grossem Geschenck verehret vnd begabet auffgenommen. IX.

DA Columbus in seiner ersten Schiffart zu Land gefahren/ hat er an dem Gestaden deß Meers ein höltzin Crucifix lassen auffrichtē/ darnach ist er in die Insel Haytin/welche er Hispaniolam nennet/kommen/ vnd mit vielen Spaniern auff das Land außgestiegen/ An demselbigen Orth ward er von dem Cacico(also nennen sie die Königsche auff jhre Spraach) welcher Guacanarillus mit Namen hieß/ gantz freundtlich vnnd herrlich auffgenommen/vnd als sie beyde einander mit Geschenck vnd Gabē verehreten/haben sie ein Bündnuß der zukünfftigen Freundtschafft mit einander gemacht vñ bestättiget: Es verehret vnnd begabet Columbus den König mit Hembdern/Hüten/Messern/ Spiegeln vnd dergleichē/ Hergegen verehret vñ schencket dem Columbo der Cacicus ein grossen vnd schweren glotzen Goldts/Capit.7.

C ij Columbus

25. *Columbus als er in India erstlich ankommen. . . .* Engraving.

25

Girolamo Benzoni

DAS VIERDTE BUCH VON DER NEUWEN WELT. ODER NEUWE UND GRÜNDTLICHE HISTORIEN, VON DEM NIDERGÄNGISCHEN INDIEN . . .

Frankfurt, 1594. Part four of Theodor de Bry, Johann Theodor de Bry, and Johann Israel de Bry, *America*, Thirteen volumes, 1593–1630

Benzoni's text describes his travels in New Spain from 1541 to 1556. First published in Venice in 1565, it is here republished in German as part four of de Bry's *Grand Voyages* to America, accompanied by a new set of illustrations which significantly reshape its narrative impact. The images, evidently not based on actual observation, emphasize Spanish cruelty in the New World. Their apparent origin in the imagination of de Bry's fervently Protestant illustrators reflects the influence of the "Black Legend" of Spanish colonization that was emerging in Protestant Northern Europe. Their polemic value helps explain why they were so frequently copied and imitated for the next two centuries. De Bry and his sons eventually published in both German and Latin a set of thirteen volumes of American voyages and another set of twelve volumes describing voyages to the Indies. A complete German edition of each set, from which the present copy is drawn, was presented by the Mellon estate to the Yale Center for British Art.

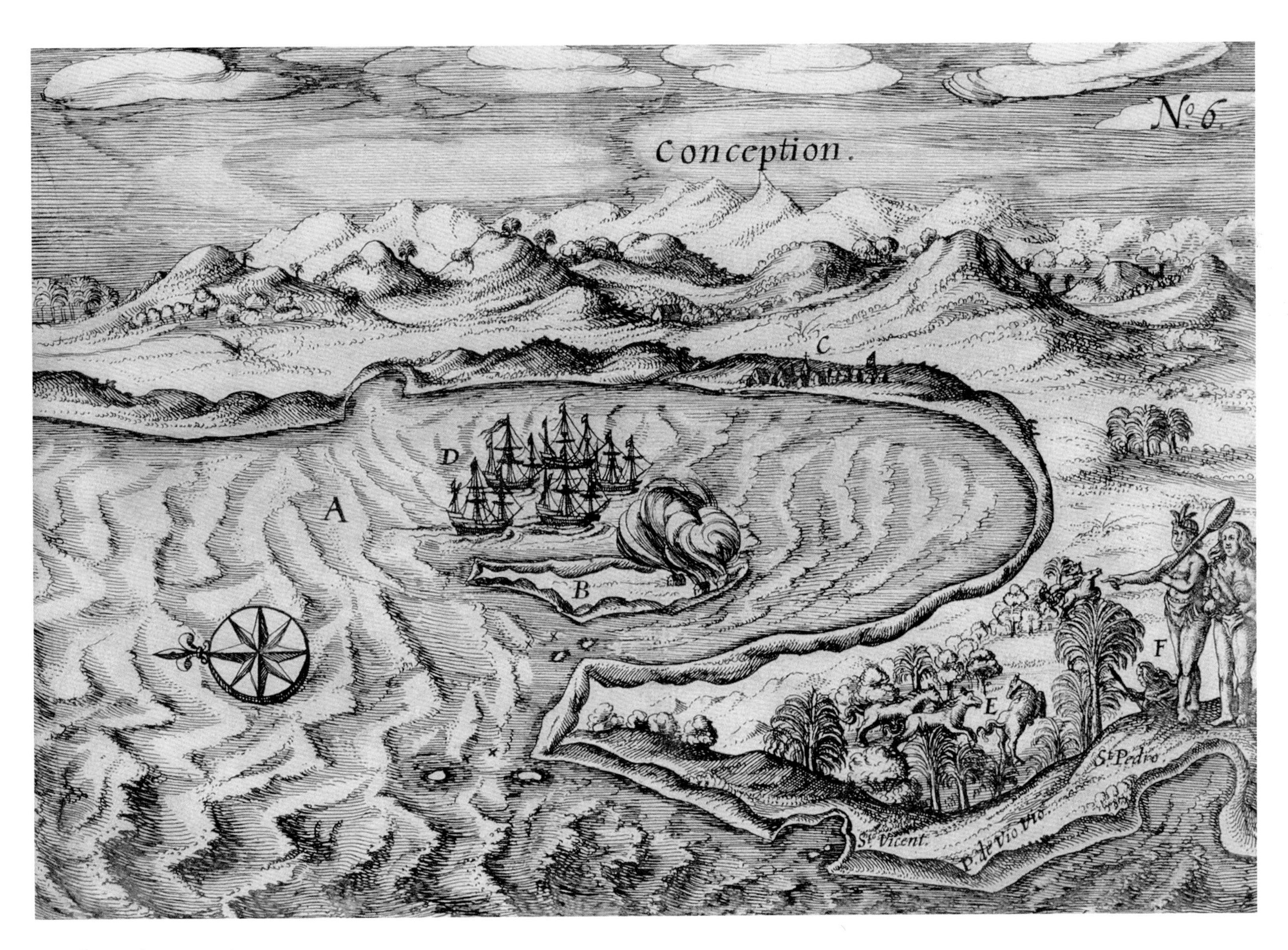

26. *Conception*. Engraving.

26
Joris van Spilbergen
MIROIR OOST & WEST-INDICAL . . .

Amsterdam, 1621

A member of the Dutch East India Company, Spilbergen was appointed the first Dutch envoy to Ceylon in 1602. A little more than a decade later, from 1614 through 1618, he completed a circumnavigation via the Strait of Magellan. His account of that trip, first published in Dutch in 1619, included twenty-five views and two maps. The views of South American ports are highly stylized but they remain interesting, for both the Spanish and Portuguese governments strictly censored information about their new world colonies and few depictions of them can be found in the printed literature of the time. Although the list of illustrations in this first French edition describes only twenty plates, the volume includes all twenty-seven images, printed from the same engraved copper plates used for the original edition.

27

John Smith

THE GENERALL HISTORIE OF VIRGINIA, NEW-ENGLAND, AND THE SUMMER ISLES . . .

London, 1624

Long before Davy Crockett and Buffalo Bill Cody, John Smith emerged as America's first self-promoted frontier "hero." Although it draws upon many contemporary sources, the *Generall Historie* relies primarily upon Smith's personal experiences in Virginia from 1606 to 1609 and his exploration of the New England coast from 1610 to 1617. A skillful publicist, Smith used pictures as well as words to establish his reputation as the savior of Virginia. He draped a graphic version of his service in Virginia around a map of the North Carolina-southern Virginia coast, adding the apparently modest but provocatively open-ended caption, "A description of part of the adventures of Cap. Smith in Virginia." The present copy was once owned by the famous Americana collector and bibliographer Thomas W. Streeter.

27. *A description of part of the adventures of Cap. Smith in Virginia.* Engraving.

Their
Idoll
A Preist
Their Coniuration about C: Smith 1607
C.Smith taketh the King of Pamavnkee prisoner 1608
A description of part of the adventures of Cap: Smith in Virginia.
The Country wee now call Virginia beginneth at Cape Henry distant from Roanoack 60 miles, where was Sr. Walter Raleigh's plantation: and because the people differ very little from them of Powhatan in any thing, I have inserted those figures in this place because of the conveniency.
Waldens Oake
Lenox rocks
Mangoack
Richmonds
steps
Howards Mountaynes
Stuards reach
Bedfords valley
Moratuck flu:
Anadales chase
Ohanoack
Ramushonoq
L: Salvage Rocke
Beauchamps playne
Chawanok flu:
Alice
Smith
foild
Metocaum
Catoking
Maraton
Mascoming
Segars grove
Chisapeack
Secota
Setuoc
Purchace Iles
Mecopen
Cotan
Cecils Harbor
Jamasqueack
Chepanu
Heriots Ile
Townsrows end
Paquinip
Laynflu:
Pasquenock
Mildmaids roade
Adams Sound
C Henry
Pomeiock
P. Corbett
P. Bacon
P. Barkley
P. Box
Ile Hatton
Roanoak
P. Goade
Arundells Ile
P. Vaughan
Eßex Ile
Worcester inlet
Greenevills rode
Hertfords Ile
C. Amidas
A Scale of 10 Leauges.
1 2 3 4 5 6 7 8 9 10
Vincere est Viuere
C.S.
King Powhatan comands C.Smith to be slayne, his daughter Pokahontas beggs his life his thankfullness and how he subiected 39 of their kings. reade ÿ history.
xtracted out of ÿ generall history of Virginia, New England, and Somer Iles, by Robert Vaughan.
printed by James Reeve

28. Untitled plate depicting an attack upon an Indian stockade. Engraving.

28

Samuel de Champlain

VOYAGES ET DESCOUVERTURES FAITES EN LA NOUVELLE FRANCE . . .

Paris, 1627

Champlain's accounts of his many voyages to North America remain the best source for the early history of New France. His first, brief account was published in 1603. A longer, illustrated narrative appeared in 1613, followed by the first edition of *Voyages et Descouvertures* in 1619. A final volume, summarizing his experiences after 1620, was first published in 1632. The images of Native American life that appear in Champlain seem faithful to his original observations, neither simplified nor embellished by the engravers. Alongside John White's depiction of the Indians around Roanoke, they are among the most reliable images of eastern Native Americans from the era of early exploration. The present copy was once owned by the noted British collector Sir Thomas Phillipps.

29

Arnoldus Montanus

DIE UNBEKANTE NEUE WELT . . .

Amsterdam, 1673

Montanus wrote several tracts concerning the Dutch East India Company's activities in China and Japan, but his history of America is a far more ambitious work. A compendium of accounts by numerous authors, it is heavily illustrated with plates representing the religious festivals, material culture, occupations, and customs of Native Americans, most of them imaginary. Despite their inaccuracies, the plates (and text) were quickly plagiarized, first in 1670 by Englishman John Ogilby and then, in this edition from 1673, by German geographer Olfert Dapper. Eight plates in this edition appear as mirror images from the first edition, suggesting that the original prints may have served as tracing masters for making new copper plates.

29. *Virginiae partis australis et Floridae partis orientalis.* Engraving.

30. *La Ville, le Château et le Village de St. Augustin, en Amerique.* Engraving.

30
Pieter van der Aa
LA GALERIE AGREABLE DU MONDE . . .

Leiden, 1729

At the beginning of the eighteenth century the Dutch publisher Pieter van der Aa issued several massive series of reprinted voyages and travels encompassing hundreds of narratives from throughout the world. At the same time he published this vastly rarer series of views, said to have been produced in only one hundred sets, collecting hundreds of city and townscapes from every continent. The Mellon set is one of the few complete examples known. The accuracy of the views varied dramatically; some of them were based on actual observation, while others stemmed from the imagination of the engravers.

31

BOUND VOLUME OF FOUR ICELANDIC SAGAS

Skalhollte, 1688

This volume contains four separate sagas, all printed in Iceland in 1688, and describing the settling of that island or the further explorations of the Norse in Greenland and beyond. They stem from a period when scholarly interest in the early sagas was reviving. The first and most important is the *Landnamabok*, a catalogue of the earliest settlers in Iceland with references to Greenland. The frontispiece of Arngrimur Jonsson's *Gronlandia Edur . . .*, largely devoted to the adventures of Eric the Red, shows that famed Viking in a suit of armor more appropriate to the era of publication than to the tenth century.

31. Frontispiece portrait of Eric the Red from the *Gronlandia Saga.* Woodcut.

32. Danes taking an Eskimo captive. Hand-colored woodcut.

32

Hinrich Rink, editor

KALADLIT OKALLUKTUALLIAIT

Godthaab, 1859–1863

Hinrich Rink was deeply interested in the folklore of the Greenland Eskimo, whose oral traditions preserved tales of the clashes with Norse settlers in Viking times. Rink collected these narratives and commissioned an Eskimo, Aron of Kangeq, to illustrate them. Aron, a sealer by trade, was a young man confined to bed by tuberculosis in a small trading station on the Davis Strait. His remarkable woodcuts, showing scenes from the bloody fights with the Norse, explore a legendary world of drama and violence set against a vast and weird landscape. They are suitable illustrations for what might be called the *Iliad* of the Greenland Eskimo.

32. Battle between Eskimos and Vikings. Hand-colored woodcut.

POK AIPANILO KAVDLUNAITUT ATORDLUTIK
PISUGTUARTUT IGDLORPAGSSUIT AKORNANE.

POK AIPANILO PISUGTUARTUT ORPIGPAGSSUIT
AKORNANE.

33. Pok visits Copenhagen. Hand-colored woodcut.

33
Pok

POK: KALALEK AVALANGNEK . . .

Godthaab, 1857

In 1857 the Danish Crown Inspector for southern Greenland, Hinrich Rink, brought a small printing press to the capital of Godthaab, on the west coast of the island. Rink hoped to use the press for both educational and governmental subjects, and installed it in a small shed behind his house. This was the first book produced there, the narrative of a Greenland Eskimo named Pok who visited Copenhagen in 1724. Charmingly illustrated with locally made woodcuts, it provides the narrative of a "native" going to visit the exotic "other" of a large European city.

34

NEU-ERÖFFNETES AMPHITHEATRUM WORINNEN III. AUS DEM GANTZEN AMERICA ALLE NATIONEN NACH IHREM HABIT IN SAUBERN FIGUREN REPRAESENTIRET . . .

Erffurth, 1723

Between 1722 and 1728, German publisher Johann Michael Funcken completed a world geography in five parts, each with its own title page and separate pagination. Volume three, published in 1723, describes America and features woodcuts intended to depict Native Americans from throughout the hemisphere. Some of the images are derived from de Bry, while the sources for others are uncertain. Utterly lacking ethnographic integrity, they nonetheless reveal much about the symbols of "Indian-ness" that had taken root in eighteenth-century European iconography.

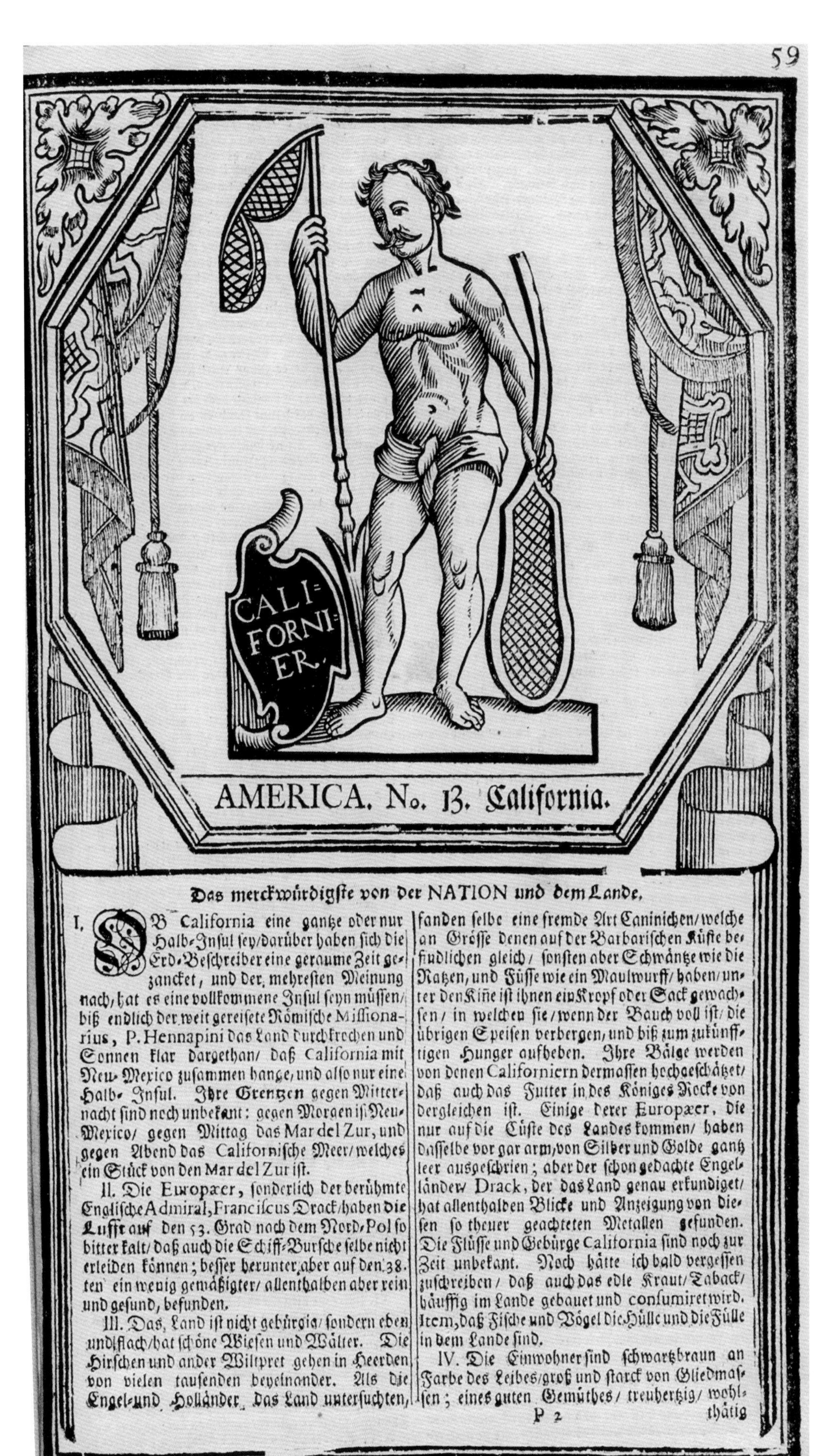
59

CALI-FORNI-ER.

AMERICA. No. 13. California.

Das merckwürdigste von der NATION und dem Lande.

I. Ob California eine gantze oder nur Halb-Insul sey/darüber haben sich die Erd-Beschreiber eine geraume Zeit gezancket, und der mehresten Meinung nach/hat es eine vollkommene Insul seyn müssen/ biß endlich der weit gereisete Römische Missionarius, P. Hennapini das Land durchkrochen und Sonnen klar dargethan/ daß California mit Neu-Mexico zusammen hange, und also nur eine Halb-Insul. Ihre Grentzen gegen Mitternacht sind noch unbekant: gegen Morgen ist Neu-Mexico/ gegen Mittag das Mar del Zur, und gegen Abend das Californische Meer/ welches ein Stück von den Mar del Zur ist.

II. Die Europæer, sonderlich der berühmte Englische Admiral, Franciscus Drack/haben die Lufft auf den 53. Grad nach dem Nord-Pol so bitter kalt/ daß auch die Schiff-Bursche selbe nicht erleiden können; besser herunter, aber auf den 38. ten ein wenig gemäßigter/ allenthalben aber rein und gesund, befunden.

III. Das Land ist nicht gebürgig/ sondern eben und flach/hat schöne Wiesen und Wälter. Die Hirschen und ander Wiltpret gehen in Heerden von vielen tausenden beyeinander. Als die Engel- und Holländer das Land untersuchten, fanden selbe eine fremde Art Caninichen/ welche an Grösse denen auf der Barbarischen Küste befindlichen gleich/ sonsten aber Schwäntze wie die Ratzen, und Füsse wie ein Maulwurff/ haben/ unter den Kiñe ist ihnen ein Kropf oder Sack gewachsen/ in welchen sie/ wenn der Bauch voll ist/ die übrigen Speisen verbergen, und biß zum zukünfftigen Hunger aufheben. Ihre Bälge werden von denen Californiern dermassen hochgeschätzet/ daß auch das Futter in des Königes Rocke von dergleichen ist. Einige derer Europæer, die nur auf die Cüste des Landes kommen/ haben dasselbe vor gar arm, von Silber und Golde gantz leer ausgeschrien; aber der schon gedachte Engelländer Drack, der das Land genau erkundiget/ hat allenthalben Blicke und Anzeigung von diesen so theuer geachteten Metallen gefunden. Die Flüsse und Gebürge California sind noch zur Zeit unbekant. Noch hätte ich bald vergessen zuschreiben/ daß auch das edle Kraut/ Taback/ häuffig im Lande gebauet und consumiret wird. Item, daß Fische und Vögel die Hülle und die Fülle in dem Lande sind.

IV. Die Einwohner sind schwartzbraun an Farbe des Leibes/ groß und starck von Gliedmassen; eines guten Gemüthes/ treuhertzig/ wohl-

P 2 thätig

34. *America. No. 13. California.*
Woodcut.

35. John Faber, *Sa Ga Yean Qua Rash Tow. King of ye Maquas. alias King Brant.* Mezzotint.

35

THE FOUR INDIAN KINGS OF CANADA

John Faber, *Sa Ga Yean Qua Rash Tow. King of ye Maquas. alias King Brant.* Mezzotint, London, 1710
John Simon, *Etow Oh Koam, King of the River Nation.* Mezzotint after a painting by John Verelst, London, ca. 1755

Even when Native Americans sat for portraits before trained artists, the "truth" of the resulting images could be a complicated matter. In 1710, a colonial official from New York, Peter Schuyler, brought four "Indian Kings" to England to meet Queen Anne. The visiting dignitaries created a stir throughout London. The Dutch artist John Verelst painted full body portraits of them from which a set of mezzotints was made. Another artist, John Faber, may also have painted the kings, but all that survives of his efforts is a set of four mezzotints. Additional prints were drawn "from life" during the Indians' visit. The portraits' remarkable detail has made them extraordinarily useful in understanding Mohawk and Mahican material culture, but the four men were almost certainly not tribal leaders as Schuyler claimed. They appear to have been four young men who, having formed friendly relations with British traders and officials, agreed to participate in a calculated effort to gain support from the Crown for military efforts against the French. Despite the deception, the images of the Indian Kings remained strong in Britain throughout the eighteenth century, and when the Seven Years' War broke out in 1755, Simon's prints were republished to reinforce the legitimacy of Britain's claims in North America.

35.
John Simon,
Etow Oh Koam, King of the River Nation.
Mezzotint after John Verelst.

36. *Habillemens des Coureurs de bois.* Wash drawing.

36

CANADIAN DRAWINGS OF BEAVER HUNTING

Eighteenth century

Although most scholarly attention is paid to public works of art, it is clear that making pictures fulfills a variety of personal as well as public needs. Private sketchbooks, like unpublished diaries, frequently capture the attitudes and interests of men and women undistinguished in any other regard. Perhaps we will never discover who made this collection of eight drawings depicting the Canadian fur industry or why he or she chose to do so. Even in their anonymity, they stand as a unique visual account of the economic activity that led Frenchmen (as well as their British and American counterparts) deep into America's interior.

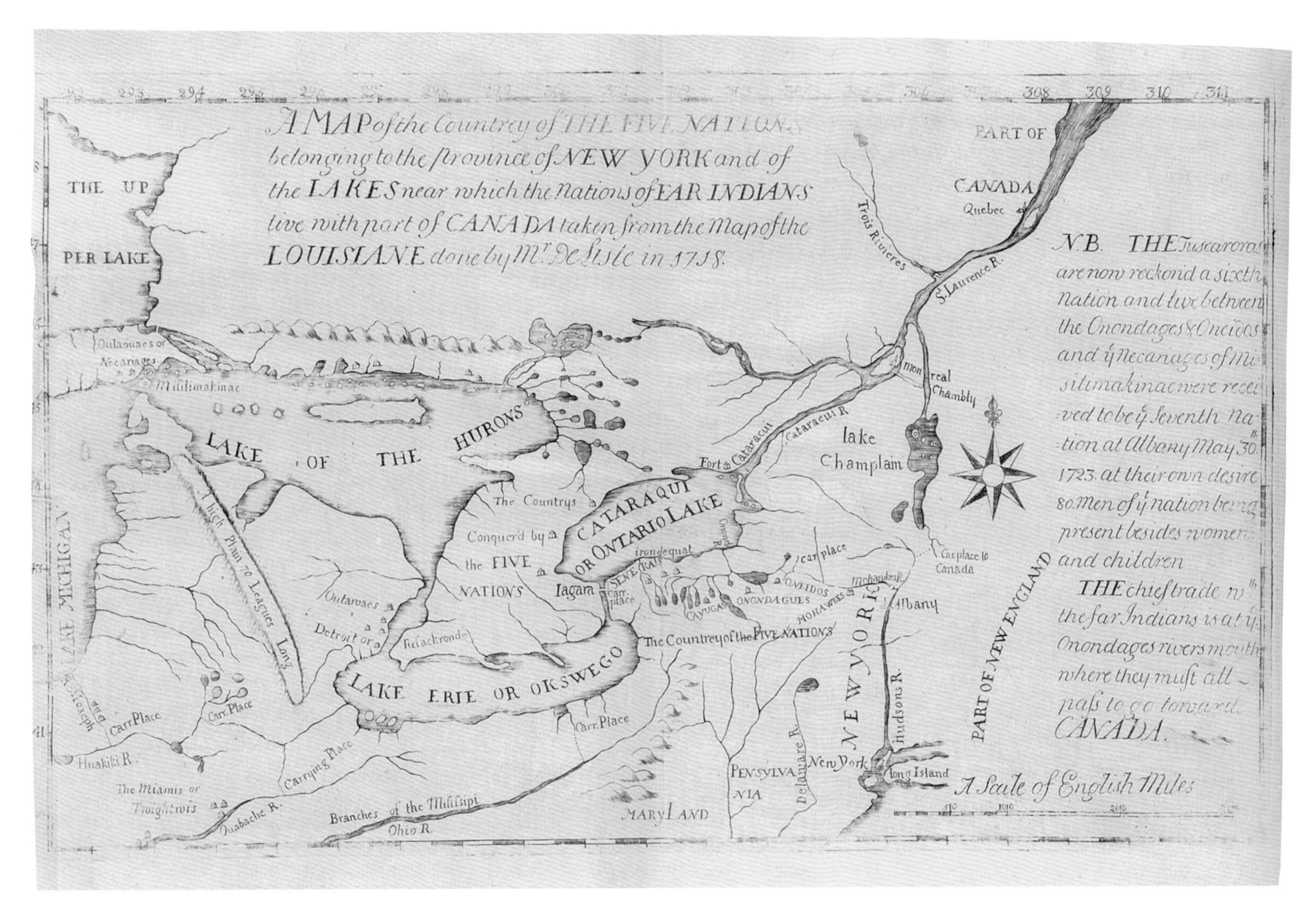

37. *A map of the Country of the Five Nations*. Engraving.

37

Cadwallader Colden

PAPERS RELATING TO AN ACT OF THE ASSEMBLY OF THE PROVINCE OF NEW-YORK, FOR ENCOURAGEMENT OF THE INDIAN TRADE, &C . . .

New York, 1724

Cadwallader Colden had lived in New York for less than four years when he published this slim volume to raise the colony's understanding of the important role the Iroquois Confederacy would play in the imperial conflict between Britain and France. A physician, natural scientist, the inventor of stereotyping, and later lieutenant governor of New York, Colden had moved to Philadelphia from Scotland in 1710. In 1720, Governor Robert Hunter appointed him surveyor general of New York. His *Map of the Country of the Five Nations*, designed to make clear the pivotal location of the Iroquois, was the first map engraved in New York, and the beginning of Colden's campaign to reshape colonial Indian policy. Addressed primarily to influence a small circle of politicians, the essay was probably issued in a relative handful of copies. It is among the rarest of early New York imprints; only three perfect copies have been identified.

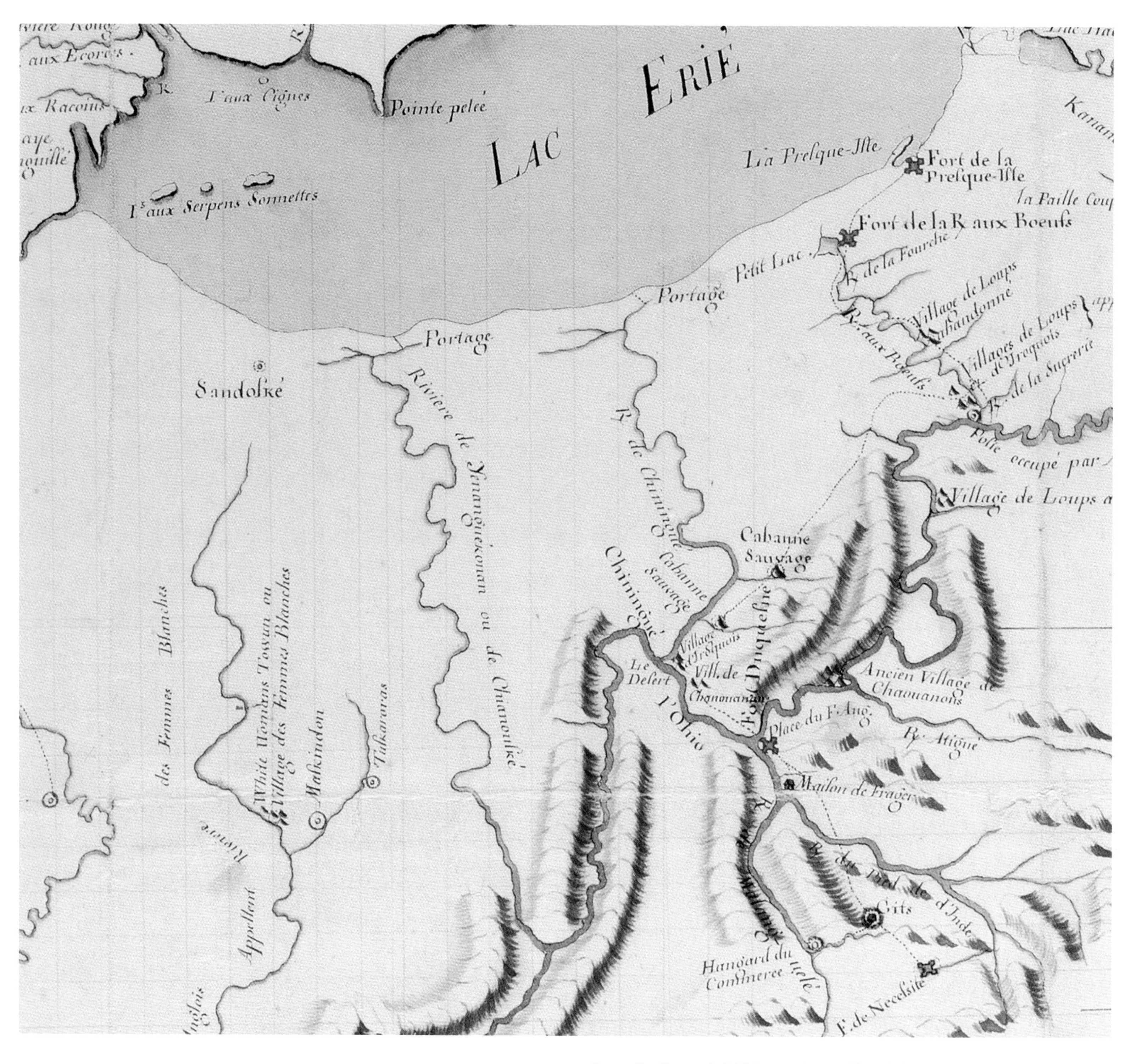

38. *Carte du Cours de L'Ohyo ou La Belle Riviere.* Hand-colored manuscript.

38

Jacques Nicolas Bellin

CARTE DU COURS DE L'OHYO OU LA BELLE RIVIERE

Paris, 1755

One of eighteenth-century France's most distinguished cartographers, Jacques Nicolas Bellin served for more than fifty years in the French Hydrographic Service. The first "Ingénieur hydrographe de la Marine" he was later appointed "Hydrographer to the King." His many maps and sea charts of all parts of the world are renowned for their beauty and accuracy. As senior engineer at the Dépot des Cartes et Plans de la Marine — the main depository of cartographic information relating to North America — Bellin drafted numerous maps including those in Charlevoix's *Histoire et description generale de la Nouvelle France* (1744) and the *Carte de l'Amerique Septentrionale depuis 28 degré de latitude jusqu'au 72* (1755). His manuscript map of the Ohio country, prepared as the Seven Years' War was unfolding, likely represents the most complete understanding that France could muster concerning the region in which the war began.

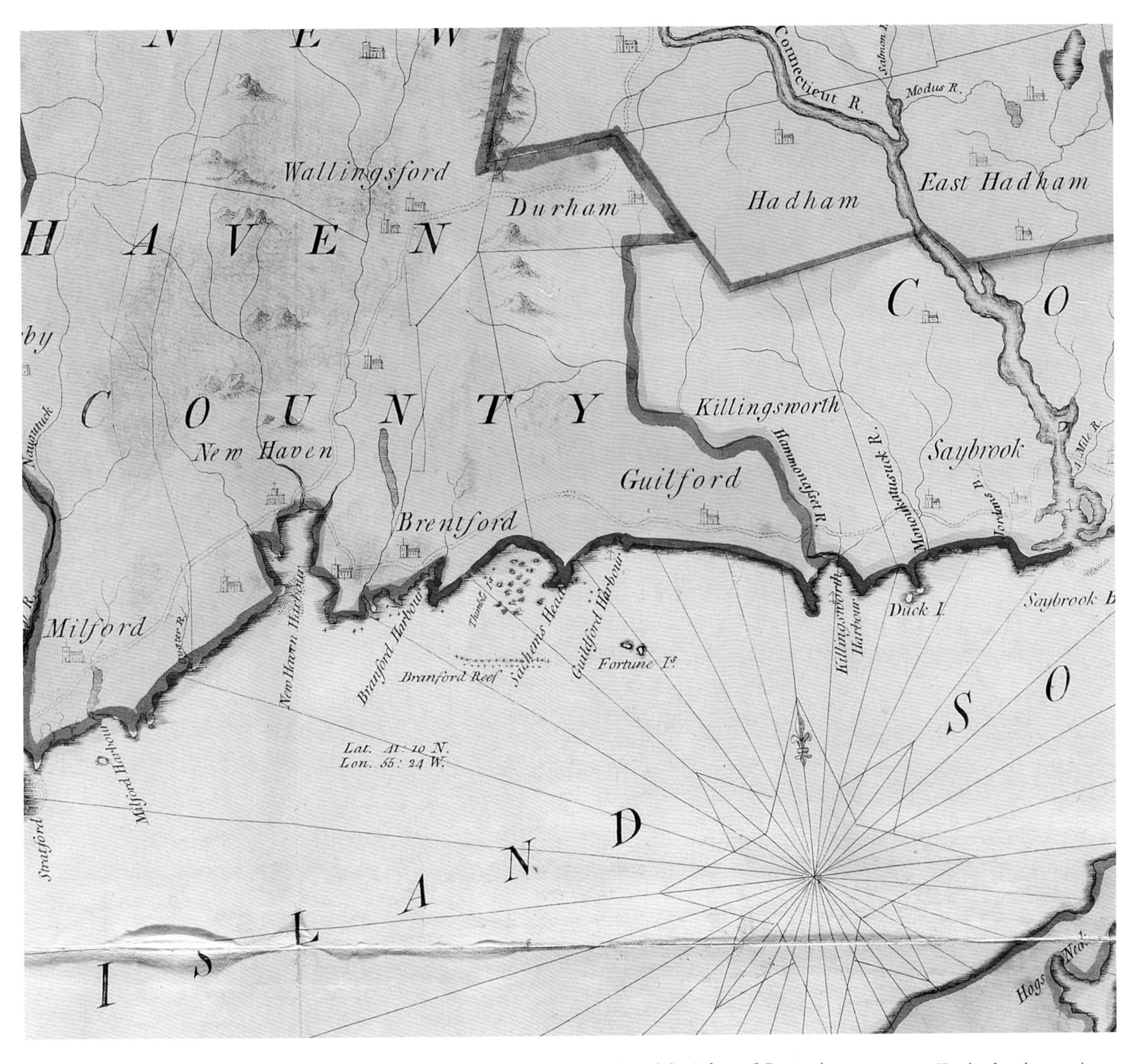

39. Moses Park, *Connecticut. . . . Plan of the Colony of Connecticut. . . .*, 1766. Hand-colored engraving

39

COMPOSITE ATLAS OF 45 AMERICAN MAPS

1722 to 1766

Amidst the imperial, revolutionary, and Indian conflicts of the eighteenth century, cartographic knowledge of the American countryside was essential for government officials, military leaders, and businessmen. The care taken in assembling this extraordinary atlas reflects the value placed upon maps. The collection includes thirteen French maps by Bellin as well as some of the earliest surveys of James Cook. Of special interest to Connecticut residents is a copy of Moses Park's rare 1766 map, the most complete map of the colony to its time. From the uniform nature of the coloring that appears on the maps, it is probable that the atlas was colored by one hand at the time of binding. As most of the maps are from the 1750s and 1760s it seems likely that the album was assembled in the late 1760s.

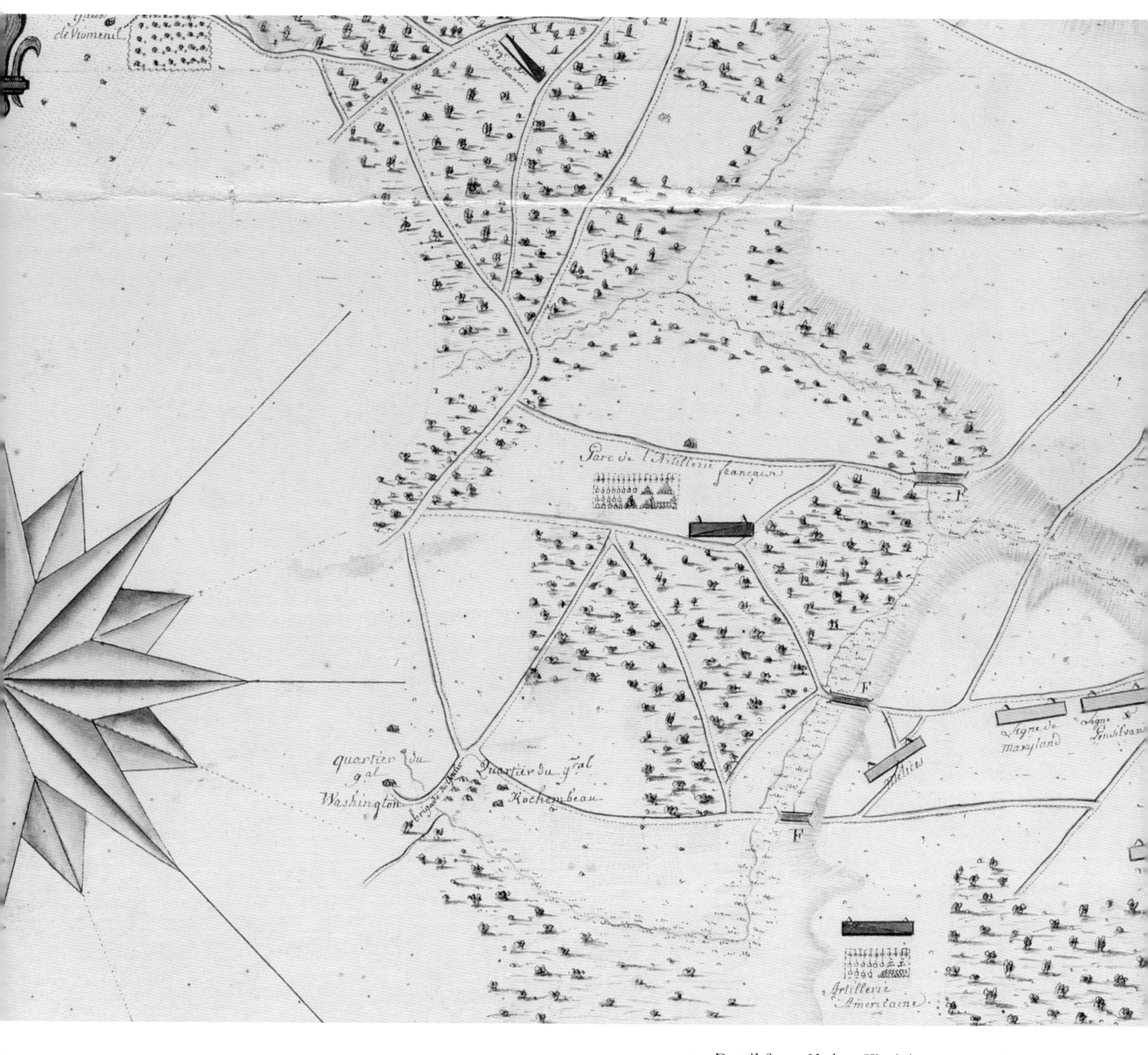

40. Detail from *York en Virginie, 1781.* Hand-colored manuscript.

40

Henri Crublier d'Opterre

MANUSCRIPTS DOCUMENTING THE FRENCH ARMY'S ROLE IN THE AMERICAN REVOLUTION

Virginia, 1781

An engineer and lieutenant-colonel in the French army during the American Revolution, Henri Crublier d'Opterre marched under the command of the Comte de Rochambeau from Newport to Yorktown, where he took part in the decisive battle of the war. His papers include not only his annotated copies of printed maps utilized by the army, but also his own manuscript maps of the campaign, including one of the mouth of Chesapeake Bay, with the positions of

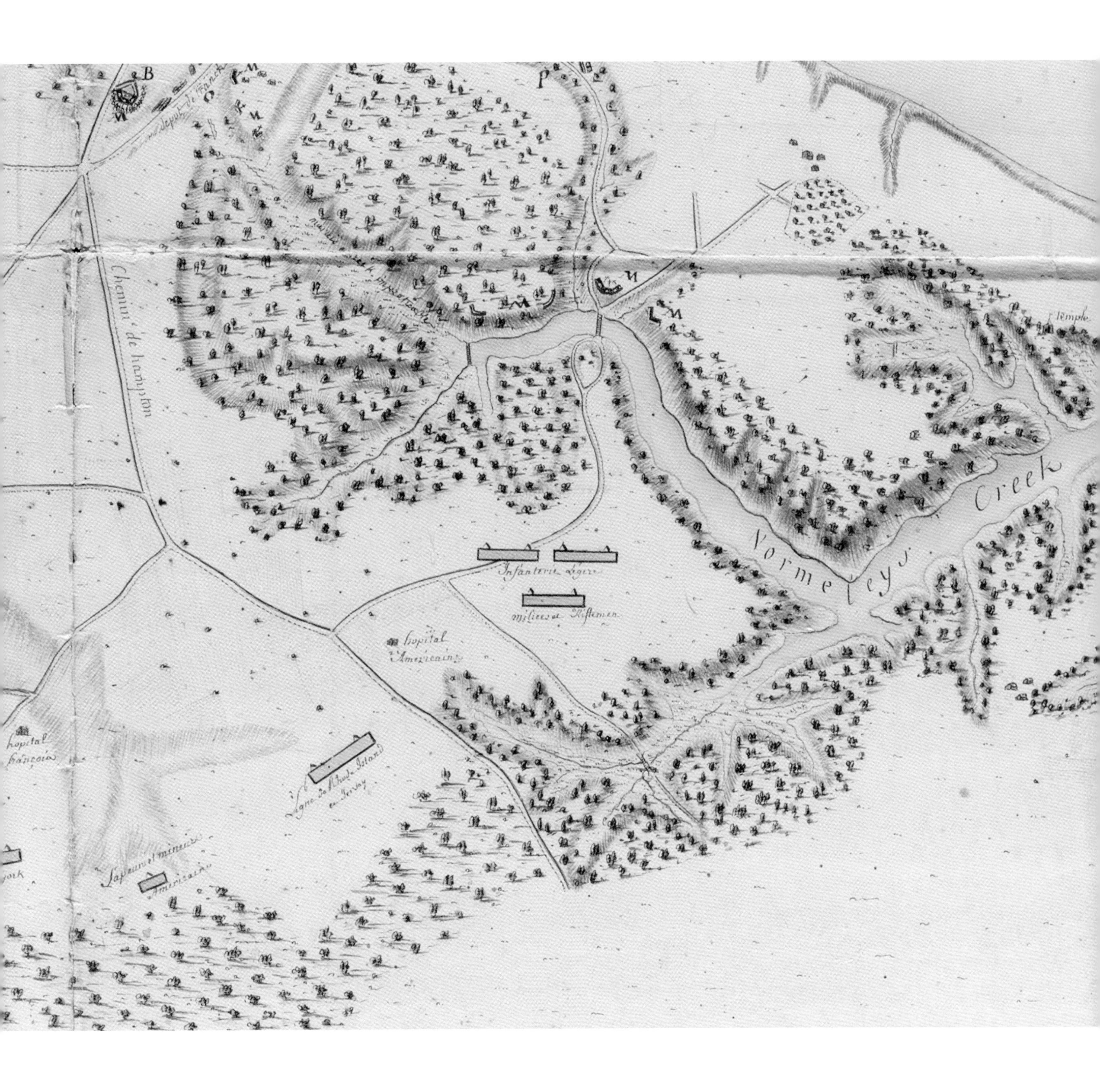

ships and troops, and another of the town of Yorktown depicting the location of the various army units. The journal that accompanies the maps includes his narrative of the siege, with a detailed critique of the British defenses. At the Beinecke Library, the Crublier d'Opterre manuscripts rejoin the papers of the Comte de Rochambeau, which Mr. Mellon presented to the library in 1992.

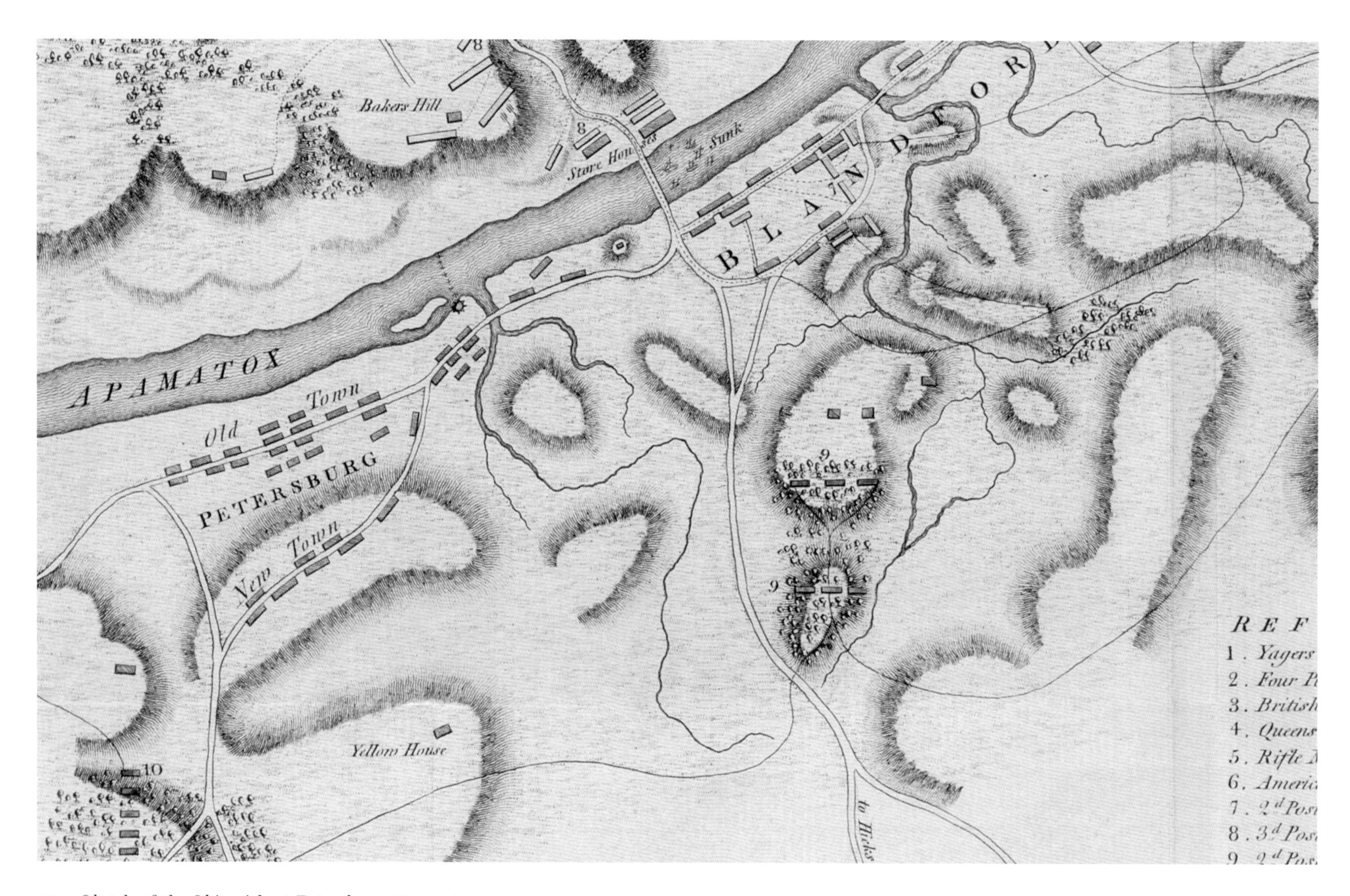

41. *Sketch of the Skirmish at Petersburg.* Engraving.

41

John Graves Simcoe

A JOURNAL OF THE OPERATIONS OF THE QUEEN'S RANGERS, FROM THE END OF THE YEAR 1777, TO THE CONCLUSION OF THE LATE AMERICAN WAR

Exeter, 1787

One of the rarest of all Revolutionary War narratives, Simcoe's account relates his leadership of a group of Loyalists who later helped found the province of Upper Canada. A twenty-three-year-old officer in the British army, Simcoe arrived in Boston in 1775 only two days after the Battle of Bunker Hill. His service in Boston, New York, and New Jersey earned him a reputation as both as a commander and military theorist. In October 1777, he was promoted to major and made regimental commander of the Queen's Rangers. The Rangers, a celebrated band of loyalists, were first recruited by Colonel Robert Rogers, who had commanded the famous Rogers' Rangers during the Seven Years' War. Under Simcoe, they helped defeat Washington at Brandywine Creek and distinguished themselves throughout the southern campaigns of 1780 and 1781. After the war Simcoe helped found Toronto and served as lieutenant governor of Upper Canada.

42

MANHATTAN ISLAND

New York, 1782–1783

Nearly nine feet long, this hand-colored map of Manhattan and its immediate environs dates from the end of the Revolutionary War. Probably executed by a British engineer, it shows New York at a time when most of Manhattan remained unsettled. Perhaps the most detailed map of the island to its time, it locates the residences of important individuals as well as roads and fortifications.

42. Manhattan Island.
Hand-colored manuscript.

NEW YORK
EAST
Fly Market Ferry
BROOKLYN FERRY
Bunkers Hill
Bowry Lane
Royal Navy Redoubt
CORLAR'S HOOK
WALLABOUT BAY
R I V

43. *A double canoe from the Sandwich Islands.* Pen, ink, and watercolor drawing.

43
Sigismund Bacstrom
DRAWINGS MADE DURING A VOYAGE AROUND THE WORLD
1791–1795

Bacstrom, a protégé of Sir Joseph Banks, had hoped to join Cook's second voyage to the Pacific but was frustrated when Banks withdrew from the expedition. In 1791 he signed aboard as surgeon on a private fur-trading ship which sailed around Cape Horn to the South Seas and Nootka Sound. Bacstrom left the ship at Nootka Sound. He later served as surgeon on several ships, visiting China and India as well as the Americas. A talented amateur artist, Bacstrom compiled an extensive portfolio of views of natives, landscapes, and ethnographic objects from the Northwest Coast of America, various Pacific islands, China, and South America. Half of the sixty-three drawings in the collection are fully rendered watercolors; others are rough sketches with detailed notes on coloring, dates of anchorage, and occasionally events on board ship or shore. Unpublished, the drawings represent an untapped source of ethnographic material.

43. *Nachey, a Chief in Norfolk Sound.* Pen, ink, and watercolor drawing.

44. *Taking Possession of a Newly Discovered Land.* Pencil and charcoal drawing.

44

George Francis Lyon

ORIGINAL SKETCHES OF THE SECOND PARRY ARCTIC EXPEDITION, 1821

George Francis Lyon sailed from England in May 1821 as commander of *HMS Hecla*, a part of William Parry's second effort to discover a Northwest Passage. An experienced naval officer, Lyon had recently returned from an expedition through northern and central Africa. Like many British military men of his time, Lyon was an accomplished topographic and portrait artist who regularly added drawings to his private journals. When the Arctic cold prevented him from using watercolors, Lyon turned to pencil and charcoal drawing. The original drawings in his notebook, now at the Yale Center for British Art, are vastly different in character from the refined prints that were eventually published by Lyon and Parry in their accounts of the expedition. Lyon made a second Arctic voyage in 1824 and subsequently passed several years in Mexico, where he again spent considerable time making sketches of local people and places.

45

Alexander von Humboldt

ATLAS GÉOGRAPHIQUE ET PHYSIQUE DU ROYAUME DE LA NOUVELLE ESPAGNE . . .

Paris, 1811

The son of a Prussian army officer and a French Huguenot mother, Alexander von Humboldt revolutionized Europe's understanding of Latin America and helped lay the foundations of modern geology and meteorology. The Napoleonic Wars prevented Humboldt from pursuing independent scientific research in Europe, but he obtained permission to visit Spain's American colonies. Between 1799 and 1804, he and his companion, French botanist Aimé Bonpland, covered more than 6,000 miles, and spent a year in close study of Mexico. For the next twenty-four years, except for brief visits to Berlin, Humboldt lived in Paris, where he found collaborators among French scientists, the greatest of his time, and engravers for the maps and illustrations that filled the thirty volumes in which he published his accumulated data. His opus, which included a wealth of material on the geography and geology of Mexico, provided the first widely available, accurate map of New Spain's northern frontiers, and its descriptions of Mexican silver mines led to widespread English investment in the mines.

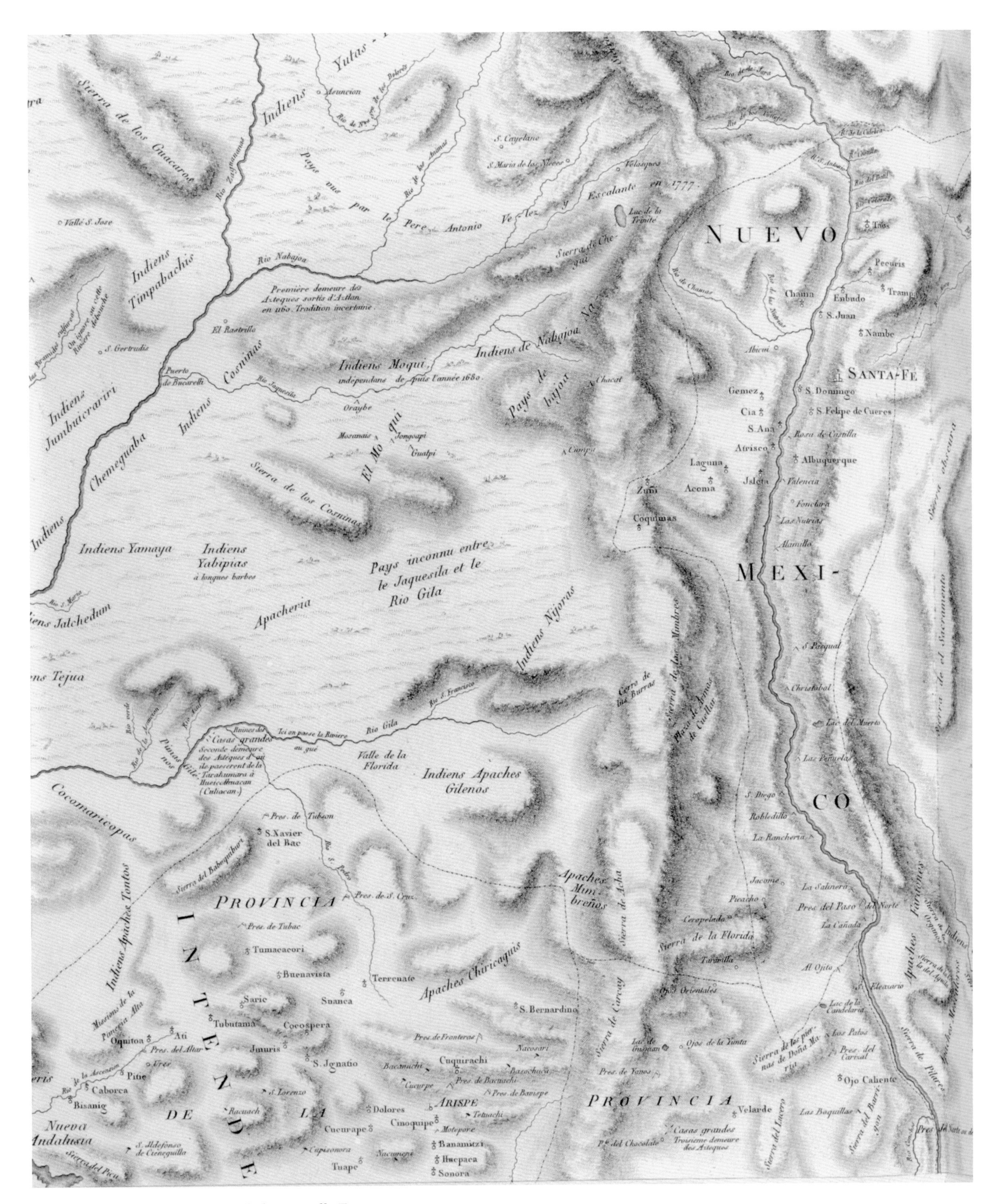

45. *Carte Générale du Royaume de la Nouvelle Espagne*.... Engraving.

A MAP OF
NORTH AMERICA,
CONSTRUCTED ACCORDING TO THE LATEST INFORMATION
by H.S.TA

46

Henry S. Tanner

THE NEW AMERICAN ATLAS . . .

Philadelphia, 1822–1823

Henry Tanner engraved his first map, a geologic map of the United States, in 1809. Over the next fifty years he became America's preeminent commercial cartographer. His *New American Atlas*, published in five folio volumes between 1819 and 1823, revolutionized American mapmaking. Comprising twenty-two large maps, several in multiple sheets, it featured the unprecedented use of a uniform scale of about fifteen miles to the inch for every state map. The "Geographical Memoir" which accompanied the atlas listed the many sources Tanner consulted to achieve a level of detail and accuracy far beyond his contemporaries. The project earned Tanner international recognition; he became one of the few Americans invited to join the Geographical Societies of London and Paris. The Mellon copy is in parts as issued, in the original paper wrappers.

46. *A Map of North America, Constructed According to the Latest Information.*
Hand-colored engraving.

47. *The Attack of the Mexicans from the Chapperal.* Hand-colored lithograph.

47
Henry Walke
NAVAL PORTFOLIO. NAVAL SCENES IN THE MEXICAN WAR

New York, 1847–1848

The Mexican War was the first war in which press coverage made extensive use of pictures. The emergence of relatively inexpensive commercial lithography coincided with the development of major news weeklies and a national curiosity about the war to produce a flood of images that appeared on everything from painted panoramas to sheet music. Serving aboard the bomb ketch *Vesuvius,* U. S. naval officer Henry Walke created one of the most important visual records of the war. As a participant in Matthew Perry's campaigns against Tuxpan and Tabasco, he found time to make a series of eight sketches of the naval and amphibious operations. Striking in their detail, the prints are among the rarest eye-witness views of the War. Few complete sets exist; the Mellon set is considered among the finest assembled. Walke continued his artistic career during the Civil War. His *Naval Scenes and Reminiscences of the Civil War in the United States, on the Southern and Western Waters* was published in 1877.

48. *Battala del Sacramento.* Hand-colored lithograph.

48

Julio Michaud y Thomas

ALBUM PINTORESCO, DE LA REPUBLICA MEXICANA

Mexico, 1848-1850

Most views of the Mexican War were produced in the United States, but Mexican artists and lithographers also attempted to record the war and its consequences. Michaud y Thomas's album of hand-colored lithographs includes six plates of the war as well as thirty-three scenes from throughout the country. Based on the work of such artists as Pierre-Frédéric Lehnert, Carl Nebel, Urbano López, and Pedro Gualdi, the *Album Pintoresco* was not only Mexico's first major color plate book, but probably the most significant one produced there throughout the nineteenth century.

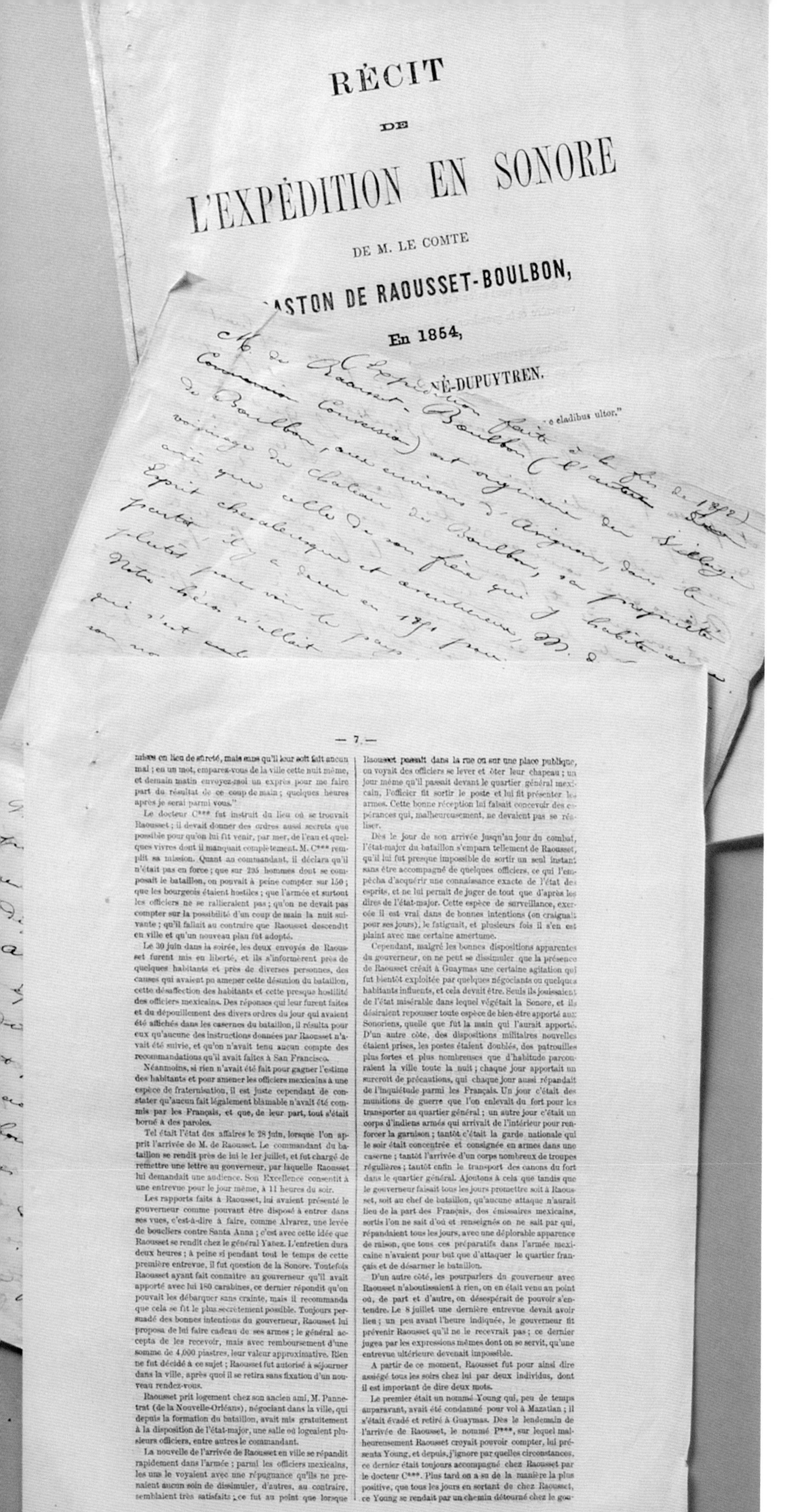

RÉCIT

DE

L'EXPÉDITION EN SONORE

DE M. LE COMTE

ASTON DE RAOUSSET-BOULBON,

En 1854,

NÉ-DUPUYTREN.

...o cladibus ultor."

— 7. —

mises en lieu de sûreté, mais sans qu'il leur soit fait aucun mal ; en un mot, emparez-vous de la ville cette nuit même, et demain matin envoyez-moi un exprès pour me faire part du résultat de ce coup de main ; quelques heures après je serai parmi vous."

Le docteur C*** fut instruit du lieu où se trouvait Raousset ; il devait donner des ordres aussi secrets que possible pour qu'on lui fit venir, par mer, de l'eau et quelques vivres dont il manquait complètement. M. C*** remplit sa mission. Quant au commandant, il déclara qu'il n'était pas en force ; que sur 235 hommes dont se composait le bataillon, on pouvait à peine compter sur 150 ; que les bourgeois étaient hostiles ; que l'armée et surtout les officiers ne se rallieraient pas ; qu'on ne devait pas compter sur la possibilité d'un coup de main la nuit suivante ; qu'il fallait au contraire que Raousset descendit en ville et qu'un nouveau plan fût adopté.

Le 30 juin dans la soirée, les deux envoyés de Raousset furent mis en liberté, et ils s'informèrent près de quelques habitants et près de diverses personnes, des causes qui avaient pu amener cette désunion du bataillon, cette désaffection des habitants et cette presque hostilité des officiers mexicains. Des réponses qui leur furent faites et du dépouillement des divers ordres du jour qui avaient été affichés dans les casernes du bataillon, il résulta pour eux qu'aucune des instructions données par Raousset n'avait été suivie, et qu'on n'avait tenu aucun compte des recommandations qu'il avait faites à San Francisco.

Néanmoins, si rien n'avait été fait pour gagner l'estime des habitants et pour amener les officiers mexicains à une espèce de fraternisation, il est juste cependant de constater qu'aucun fait légalement blâmable n'avait été commis par les Français, et que, de leur part, tout s'était borné à des paroles.

Tel était l'état des affaires le 28 juin, lorsque l'on apprit l'arrivée de M. de Raousset. Le commandant du bataillon se rendit près de lui le 1er juillet, et fut chargé de remettre une lettre au gouverneur, par laquelle Raousset lui demandait une audience. Son Excellence consentit à une entrevue pour le jour même, à 11 heures du soir.

Les rapports faits à Raousset, lui avaient présenté le gouverneur comme pouvant être disposé à entrer dans ses vues, c'est-à-dire à faire, comme Alvarez, une levée de boucliers contre Santa Anna ; c'est avec cette idée que Raousset se rendit chez le général Yañez. L'entretien dura deux heures ; à peine si pendant tout le temps de cette première entrevue, il fut question de la Sonore. Toutefois Raousset ayant fait connaître au gouverneur qu'il avait apporté avec lui 180 carabines, ce dernier répondit qu'on pouvait les débarquer sans crainte, mais il recommanda que cela se fit le plus secrètement possible. Toujours persuadé des bonnes intentions du gouverneur, Raousset lui proposa de lui faire cadeau de ses armes ; le général accepta de les recevoir, mais avec remboursement d'une somme de 4,000 piastres, leur valeur approximative. Rien ne fut décidé à ce sujet ; Raousset fut autorisé à séjourner dans la ville, après quoi il se retira sans fixation d'un nouveau rendez-vous.

Raousset prit logement chez son ancien ami, M. Pannetrat (de la Nouvelle-Orléans), négociant dans la ville, qui depuis la formation du bataillon, avait mis gratuitement à la disposition de l'état-major, une salle où logeaient plusieurs officiers, entre autres le commandant.

La nouvelle de l'arrivée de Raousset en ville se répandit rapidement dans l'armée ; parmi les officiers mexicains, les uns le voyaient avec une répugnance qu'ils ne prenaient aucun soin de dissimuler, d'autres, au contraire, semblaient très satisfaits ; ce fut au point que lorsque Raousset passait dans la rue ou sur une place publique, on voyait des officiers se lever et ôter leur chapeau ; un jour même qu'il passait devant le quartier général mexicain, l'officier fit sortir le poste et lui fit présenter les armes. Cette bonne réception lui faisait concevoir des espérances qui, malheureusement, ne devaient pas se réaliser.

Dès le jour de son arrivée jusqu'au jour du combat, l'état-major du bataillon s'empara tellement de Raousset, qu'il lui fut presque impossible de sortir un seul instant sans être accompagné de quelques officiers, ce qui l'empêcha d'acquérir une connaissance exacte de l'état des esprits, et ne lui permit de juger de tout que d'après les dires de l'état-major. Cette espèce de surveillance, exercée il est vrai dans de bonnes intentions (on craignait pour ses jours), le fatiguait, et plusieurs fois il s'en est plaint avec une certaine amertume.

Cependant, malgré les bonnes dispositions apparentes du gouverneur, on ne peut se dissimuler que la présence de Raousset créait à Guaymas une certaine agitation qui fut bientôt exploitée par quelques négociants ou quelques habitants influents, et cela devait être. Seuls ils jouissaient de l'état misérable dans lequel végétait la Sonore, et ils désiraient repousser toute espèce de bien-être apporté aux Sonoriens, quelle que fût la main qui l'aurait apporté. D'un autre côte, des dispositions militaires nouvelles étaient prises, les postes étaient doublés, des patrouilles plus fortes et plus nombreuses que d'habitude parcouraient la ville toute la nuit ; chaque jour apportait un surcroît de précautions, qui chaque jour aussi répandait de l'inquiétude parmi les Français. Un jour c'était des munitions de guerre que l'on enlevait du fort pour les transporter au quartier général ; un autre jour c'était un corps d'indiens armés qui arrivait de l'intérieur pour renforcer la garnison ; tantôt c'était la garde nationale qui le soir était concentrée et consignée en armes dans une caserne ; tantôt l'arrivée d'un corps nombreux de troupes régulières ; tantôt enfin le transport des canons du fort dans le quartier général. Ajoutons à cela que tandis que le gouverneur faisait tous les jours promettre soit à Raousset, soit au chef de bataillon, qu'aucune attaque n'aurait lieu de la part des Français, des émissaires mexicains, sortis l'on ne sait d'où et renseignés on ne sait par qui, répandaient tous les jours, avec une déplorable apparence de raison, que tous ces préparatifs dans l'armée mexicaine n'avaient pour but que d'attaquer le quartier français et de désarmer le bataillon.

D'un autre côté, les pourparlers du gouverneur avec Raousset n'aboutissaient à rien, on en était venu au point où, de part et d'autre, on désespérait de pouvoir s'entendre. Le 8 juillet une dernière entrevue devait avoir lieu ; un peu avant l'heure indiquée, le gouverneur fit prévenir Raousset qu'il ne le recevrait pas ; ce dernier jugea par les expressions mêmes dont on se servit, qu'une entrevue ultérieure devenait impossible.

A partir de ce moment, Raousset fut pour ainsi dire assiégé tous les soirs chez lui par deux individus, dont il est important de dire deux mots.

Le premier était un nommé Young qui, peu de temps auparavant, avait été condamné pour vol à Mazatlan ; il s'était évadé et retiré à Guaymas. Dès le lendemain de l'arrivée de Raousset, le nommé P***, sur lequel malheureusement Raousset croyait pouvoir compter, lui présenta Young, et depuis, j'ignore par quelles circonstances, ce dernier était toujours accompagné chez Raousset par le docteur C***. Plus tard on a su de la manière la plus positive, que tous les jours en sortant de chez Raousset, ce Young se rendait par un chemin détourné chez le gou-

49

J. B. Pigné-Dupuytren

RÉCIT DE L'EXPÉDITION EN SONORE DE M. LE COMTE GASTON DE RAOUSSET-BOULBON

San Francisco, 1854

Gaston Raoux, Comte de Raousset-Boulbon, was a young French nobleman and soldier of fortune who traveled to California to dig gold but quickly became entranced by the idea of establishing a French colony in Sonora, ostensibly to "protect" Mexico from American filibusters. He mounted two expeditions into Mexico, the first under cover of an agreement with the President of Mexico to fight Apaches. During his second expedition he fought and lost a battle with the Mexican army at Guymas and was executed before a firing squad. The Mellon copy of Pigné-Dupuytren's account of the expeditions is accompanied by a manuscript letter concerning the count and a lithographic portrait made by the San Francisco firm of Britton and Rey.

49. Pamphlet and manuscript letter.

50

LIBERTÉ. INDÉPENDANCE. EMPIRE D'HAITI

New York, 1852

This extremely rare volume (only three copies are located in the United States) records one of the many political coups that marked Haitian history in the nineteenth century. Faustin-Élie Soulouque was born a slave in French-controlled Haiti. A participant in the successful revolt of 1803 that expelled the French, he became a career officer in the Haitian army. In 1847 a group of mulatto leaders who believed they could control Soulouque engineered his appointment as president. Two years later, however, he ousted his backers and created a following of his own. He adopted the title of emperor and ruled as Faustin I. The twelve lithographs that comprise the volume depict his coronation, family members, and officials of his government. In 1859 Soulouque was deposed by his chief of staff. He escaped, but died in exile.

50. *Faustin 1er, Empereur d'Haiti.* Lithograph.

51. Untitled view of boy with bow and arrow. Engraving.

52

Ferdinand Pettrich

PORTRAITS OF DISTINGUISHED INDIANS FROM SEVERAL TRIBES, WHO VISITED WASHINGTON IN 1837 . . .

Baltimore, 1842

In 1837 the Van Buren administration brought to Washington leading chiefs of the Yankton and Santee Sioux tribes and representatives of the Sac and Fox and Iowa nations, in an attempt to make peace between the Sioux and the many tribes in Iowa and Minnesota who were their bitter enemies. Many of the Indians attending were painted by Charles Bird King as part of his famous series of portraits. They were also portrayed by another artist in Washington, the German sculptor Ferdinand Pettrich, who was at work on his models for statues to adorn the west front of the U.S. Capitol (these were rejected the following year). Pettrich supposedly first executed the portraits life-size on the walls of his Washington studio, later reducing them for this publication.

51

Felix O. C. Darley

SCENES IN INDIAN LIFE . . .

Philadelphia, 1843

One of America's most prolific illustrators of the nineteenth century, Felix Darley was born in Philadelphia in 1822. His earliest publications were in the *Saturday Museum*, then under the editorship of Edgar Allen Poe. By 1841 Darley had secured employment as staff illustrator for *Graham's Lady's and Gentleman's Magazine. Scenes in Indian Life* was Darley's first book-length piece. Done in the outline style he frequently employed, it was sold by subscription in five installments, beginning in April 1843. Although it was not based on any observation of actual Indians, its story of "noble savages" became a commercial success and was quickly reproduced in the *U.S. Democratic Review*. The ethnohistorian John C. Ewers remarked that for over forty years "Darley's Indians were seen more often in widely read American books and magazines than were the Indian pictures of any other artist." The Mellon copy is in five parts with their original paper wrappers.

52. Untitled page of Indian silhouettes. Tinted lithograph.

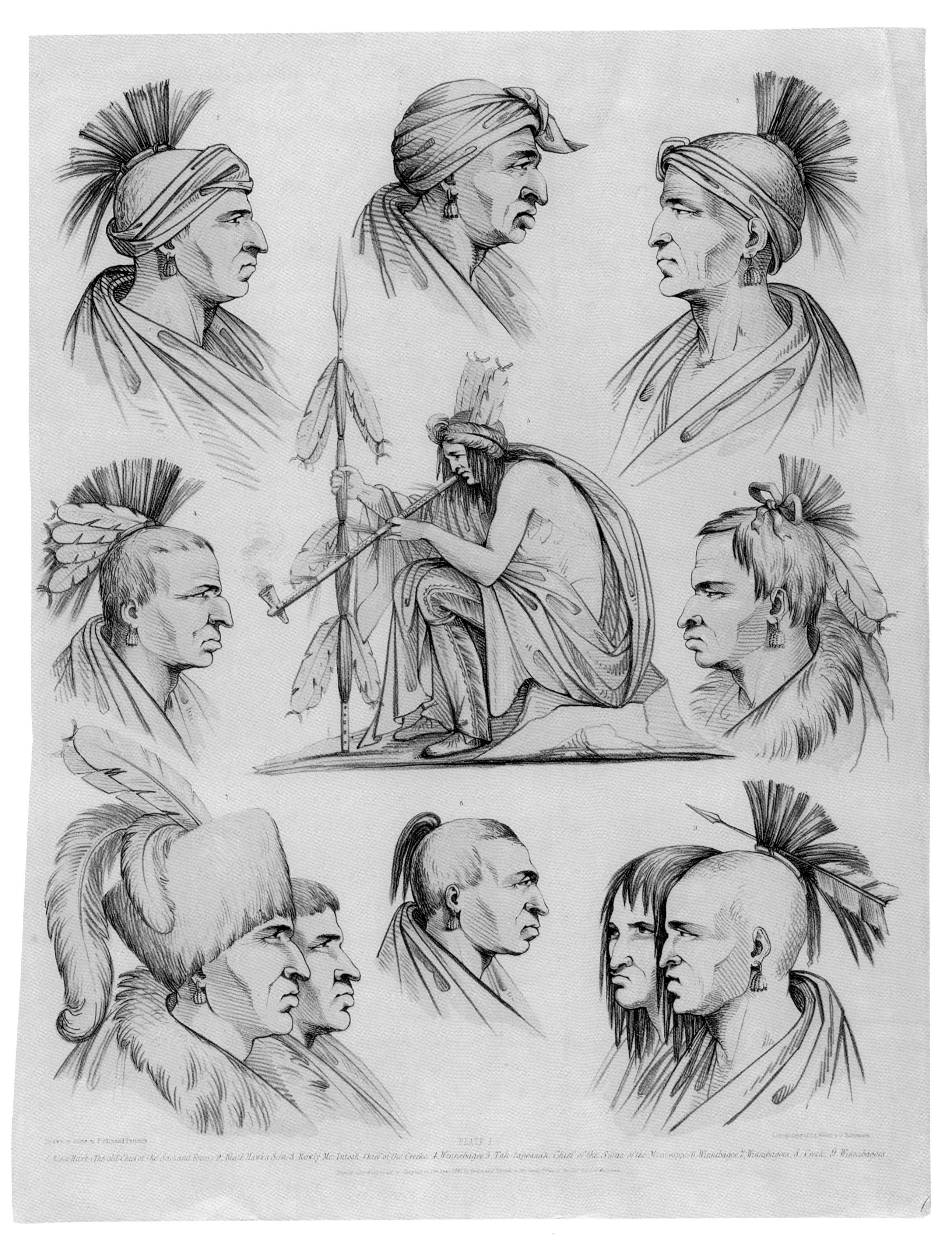
PLATE I
1. Black Hawk (The old Chief of the Sacs and Foxes) 2. Black Hawks Son. 3. Rowly Mc Intosh. Chief of the Creeks. 4. Winnebagoe. 5. Tah-tapesaah. Chief of the Sioux of the Mississippi. 6. Winnibagoe. 7. Winnibagoes. 8. Creek. 9. Winnebagoes.

53. *Tens-Kwau-Ta-Waw, The Prophet.* Hand-colored lithograph.

54

James Otto Lewis

THE NORTH AMERICAN ABORIGINAL PORTFOLIO

New York, 1844

Lewis was the first artist to execute and publish a series of portraits of North American Indians, based on paintings made while accompanying Gov. Lewis Cass of Michigan on trips around the Great Lakes from 1825 to 1827. When published in its folio format in 1835-36, it was one of the most ambitious color plate books undertaken in the United States up to that time. Shortly thereafter, the far superior McKenney and Hall publication supplanted his work. Lewis, whose artistic ability was limited, struggled unsuccessfully for years to issue a smaller quarto edition. This is the second of his failed efforts, a rare footnote to the history of Native American portraiture.

53

Thomas Loraine McKenney and James Hall

HISTORY OF THE INDIAN TRIBES OF NORTH AMERICA

Philadelphia, 1847–1850, with the original publisher's contract

This was one of the most popular American color plate books of the nineteenth century. Although Thomas McKenney, the former Commissioner of Indian Affairs, conceived of the project and worked tirelessly to bring it to fruition, he was not its author in the regular sense. The plates were based on the original paintings by Charles Bird King (a few were drawn from other artists) and the text was by the prolific James Hall of Cincinnati. After the large folio edition of 1837-42, this less expensive octavo edition was published in 1848, and was subsequently reprinted many times. The Mellon copy is accompanied by the original contract between McKenney and the publisher, James T. Bowen of Philadelphia.

54. *Kaa-Nun-der-Waaguinse-Zoo. The Berry Picker.* Hand-colored lithograph.

KAA-NUN-DER-WAAGUINSE-ZOO.
or the
BERRY PICKER.
A famous Chippewa Chief.
Painted at the Treaty of Prairie du Chien North America by J.O. Lewis
E. Jones, Lith. N.Y.

55. Untitled portrait of an Indian dancer. Hand-colored lithograph.

55

George Catlin

ILLUSTRATIONS OF THE MANNERS, CUSTOMS, AND CONDITION OF THE NORTH AMERICAN INDIANS . . .

London, 1848

The publication history of George Catlin's illustrated works about North American Indians reflects the many issues confronting nineteenth-century artists, authors, printers, and publishers as they tried to market their wares. Catlin first established a New York gallery to sell original art. His disappointing results led him to London, where his gallery became a popular attraction but not a commercial success. In 1841 he published *Letters and Notes on the Manners, Customs, and Condition of the North American Indians*, which included some 400 uncolored illustrations based on his paintings. The book quickly went through several editions and was soon translated into Swedish and German, but it never attained the success that Catlin, as publisher, hoped to achieve. Eventually, the British publishing firm of Henry Bohn acquired all of Catlin's rights. Bohn changed the title of Catlin's work, and besides the regular edition, offered hand-colored copies at ten guineas each. This practice began with the fifth edition and continued until the tenth, published in 1866. The Mellon copy is the seventh edition.

56. *Thunderstorm (Big Sewell Mountain)*. Lithograph.

56

J. Nep Roesler

WAR SCENES SKETCHED AND DRAWN ON STONE . . .

Cincinnati, 1862

Roesler, probably a trained lithographer who worked for one of Cincinnati's many printing firms, served as a corporal during the Union Army's campaign in West Virginia in the fall and winter of 1861. Like Henry Walke, Roesler captured his military experience in pictures rather than words. Upon his return to Cincinnati, he created his own lithographic stones and published a graphic memoir of his life in the army. Despite its lack of written text, no illustrated work of American history so fully expresses the experiences and emotions of the events it depicts.

Utility

Practical illustration, from technical manuals to advertising, found a variety of expressions in American publications in the national period. Such images ranged from collections of machine tool drawings to lavish chromolithographic albums of the types of wine grapes grown in California.

The earliest technical illustrations widely published in the United States were architectural, reflecting the demands of a rapidly building nation. For the most part these were pattern books giving practical guidance to carpenters at work, often pirated from British originals. A. J. Davis' *Views of the Public Buildings in the City of New York*, however, can claim to be the first native work of pure architecture. Works on American natural history were popular with the book-buying public in the United States throughout the nineteenth century, and were the best supported of the different genres of expensive illustrated works. The usable and the enumerative found a wide audience.

At the same time, elaborate illustrated publications promoted guns, clothing, and merchandising. George Catlin's rarest work is his portfolio of six plates designed to demonstrate the efficiency of Colt firearms. In an ingenious directory of merchants, Julio Rae of Philadelphia showed every storefront on what was then called Chesnut Street, accompanied by advertisements from the businesses depicted. Cuban sugar growers trumpeted the health of their industry in an elaborate and costly album. Advances in American technology found uses as well, in Louis Prang's remarkable feats of color printing, or in the use of lithography to publish the texts on the Rosetta Stone when no type fonts were available. Utility shaped illustration, and provided a text for the practical and the promotional.

57

Abraham Swan

THE BRITISH ARCHITECT . . .

Philadelphia, 1775

This elegant folio is the first architectural work to be published in America, all the more surprising as a premier effort for being issued on the eve of the Revolution. Its publisher, Robert Bell, was an innovative generalist who also ran a lending library and book auctions, and would publish *Common Sense* the next year. The book is a reprint without alteration of a well-known publication by an English carpenter and joiner, first issued in London in 1745. Despite the sweeping title, it is far more a pattern book for structural carpentry and decorative details than a grand work of design.

57. Untitled design for a façade. Engraving.

58. *Square Pavillion with Two Rings to be Roofed In.* Engraving.

59. Masonic binding for Samuel Webb.
Dyed sheep stamped in gilt.

58

William Pain

THE CARPENTER'S POCKET DIRECTORY . . .

Philadelphia, 1797

One of the most successful eighteenth-century English authors of manuals for builders and carpenters was William Pain. Four of his ten books were reprinted in the United States before 1800, and they heavily influenced the first American author of architectural works, Asher Benjamin. At the beginning of the nineteenth century, no authority was more widely available to American craftsmen. Pain's emphasis was on practical carpentry, but he also provided floor plans, elevations, and patterns for elaborate decorative elements. Surprisingly, besides the standard Palladian designs, he offered several in a Gothic style.

59

Peter Nicholson

THE CARPENTER'S NEW GUIDE . . .

Philadelphia, 1818

In the early nineteenth century the many works of the British joiner Peter Nicholson became the architectural design books most widely reprinted in the United States. The Mellon copy is notable for its elegant, elaborate presentation binding of polished sheep, stamped in gilt with Masonic designs for Samuel Webb of the Grand Lodge of Pennsylvania. Identified as an "architect" on the binding, Webb is styled a "carpenter" in the city directory of 1820, the year of the presentation, suggesting the ambivalent status of class and profession in the building trades at the time.

GRAND LODGE OF
PENNSYLVANIA
1,8 2,0.
SAMUEL WEBB.
ARCHITECT

60

Alexander Jackson Davis

VIEWS OF THE PUBLIC BUILDINGS IN THE CITY OF NEW-YORK

New York, 1826–1838

One of the most important native American architects of the early national period was A. J. Davis, educated as an artist and a lithographer, and schooled as an architect with Ithiel Town of New Haven. Davis first made his mark by designing James Hillhouse's mansion at the present site of the Kline Biology tower on the Yale campus, but his commercial practice developed mainly in New York. In this large folio, his skill at rendering façades combined with his training as a lithographer to produce the most striking and forceful work of architecture to be published in America up to that time. Davis had hoped to issue a book in multiple parts, each devoted to a different city of the United States, but only twelve plates devoted to New York were printed, and the book was never actually published.

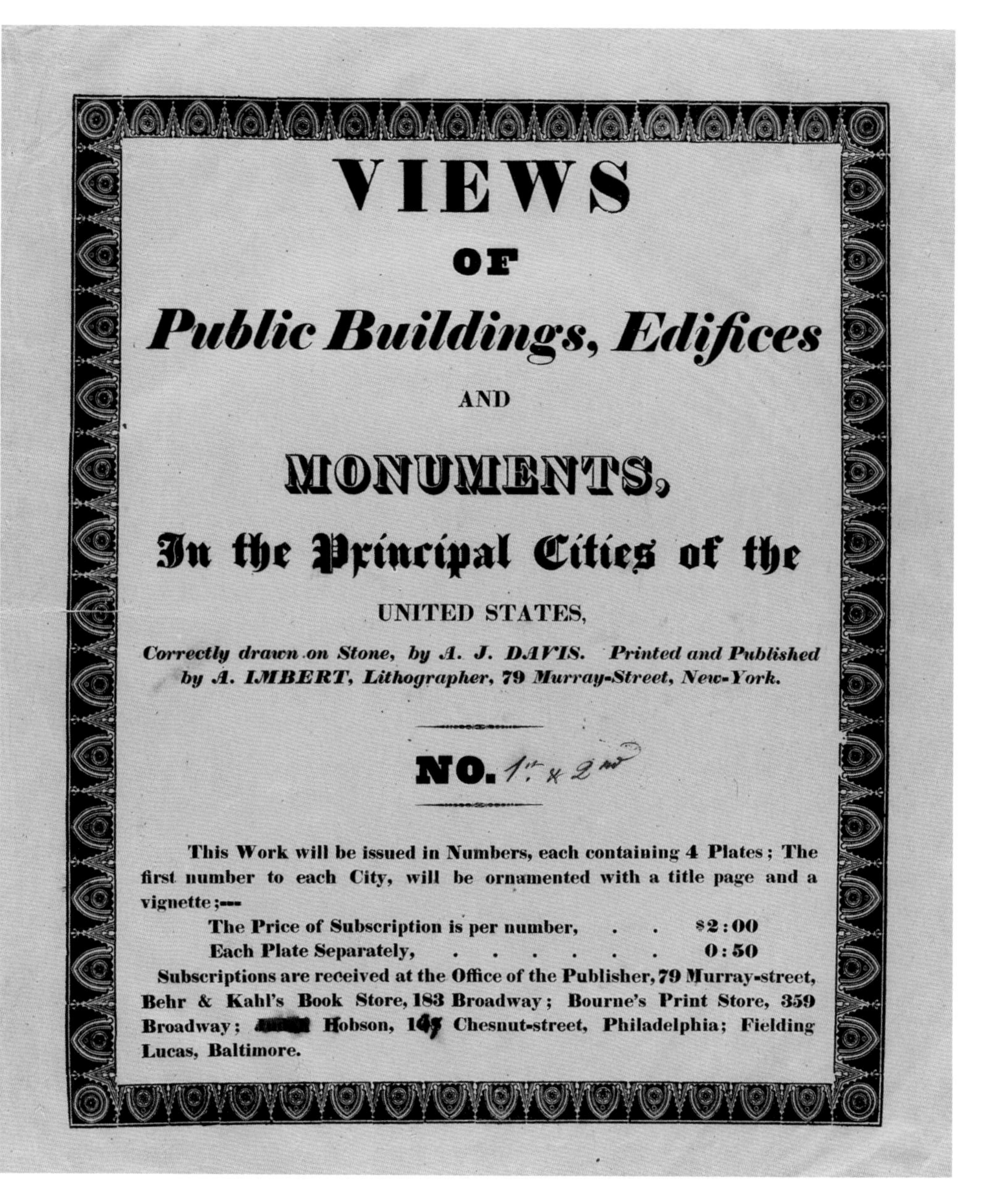

VIEWS

OF

Public Buildings, Edifices

AND

MONUMENTS,

In the Principal Cities of the

UNITED STATES,

Correctly drawn on Stone, by A. J. DAVIS. Printed and Published by A. IMBERT, Lithographer, 79 Murray-Street, New-York.

NO. 1st & 2nd

This Work will be issued in Numbers, each containing 4 Plates; The first number to each City, will be ornamented with a title page and a vignette;—

The Price of Subscription is per number, . .	$2:00
Each Plate Separately, ...	0:50

Subscriptions are received at the Office of the Publisher, 79 Murray-street, Behr & Kahl's Book Store, 183 Broadway; Bourne's Print Store, 359 Broadway; [illegible] Hobson, 14[illegible] Chesnut-street, Philadelphia; Fielding Lucas, Baltimore.

60. Paper wrapper for parts one and two. Letterpress.

60. *Masonic Hall.* Lithograph.

61. *Unio Subtentus.* Hand-colored engraving.

61

Thomas Say

AMERICAN CONCHOLOGY . . .

New Harmony, Indiana, 1830–1838

Say was a prominent naturalist, already famous for his work on American insects and his participation in Major Stephen Long's expedition to explore the Great Plains, when he joined other notable American scientists in Robert Owen's utopian experiment at New Harmony, Indiana. Here he undertook publication of his work on American fresh-water shells. The text and plates were printed at the New Harmony School Press, and the plates colored by a team of nine students. Few works of such scientific importance have been so elegantly produced in such pioneer circumstances. The Mellon copy is bound with four additional related New Harmony imprints.

62. *Point of Maine Exhibiting the Disposition of Red Sandstone Limestone and Greenstone Trap.* Hand-colored lithograph.

62
Charles T. Jackson

FIRST REPORT ON THE GEOLOGY OF THE STATE OF MAINE

Augusta, 1837

A Harvard-trained medical doctor, Jackson abandoned medicine in 1836 to establish a commercial chemistry laboratory in Boston, where he engaged in chemical, mineralogical, and geological analysis for mining and other interests. Over the next decade he emerged as one of America's leading geologists, becoming the first state geologist in Maine, New Hampshire, and Rhode Island. He carried out geological studies in Michigan for the Lake Superior Copper Company, and in 1847 was appointed U.S. geologist to conduct a survey of the Lake Superior area. Jackson's reports, which emphasized his chemical and mineralogical interests and the practical and economic inclinations of his government sponsors, made extensive use of both topographic and scientific illustration to clarify and expand the written text, a practice that became standard for virtually all nineteenth-century American geological surveys.

63

Jean Louis R. Agassiz

LAKE SUPERIOR: ITS PHYSICAL CHARACTER, VEGETATION, AND ANIMALS . . .

Boston, 1850

Agassiz came to the United States in 1846, when John Amory Lowell, cotton manufacturer and head of the Lowell Institute, invited him to deliver a course of lectures at the institute, the exemplar of popular culture in New England. A protégé of Humboldt, Agassiz had already established himself as a leading botanist, paleontologist, and glacial geologist. He took New England and America by storm. In 1847 he was appointed professor of zoology and geology at Harvard's newly established Lawrence Scientific School. *Lake Superior* was Agassiz's first major American publication. In addition to a series of uncolored topographic lithographs inserted throughout the text, the volume included a series of natural history plates as an appendix. The Mellon copy is one of the few issued in which these plates are hand-colored.

63. Lepidoptera and shells of Lake Superior.
Hand-colored lithograph.

64. *Coloring of Flowers.* Hand-colored lithograph.

64
Anne Hill
DRAWING BOOK OF FLOWERS AND FRUIT . . .

Philadelphia, 1844

This is one of the rarest American works to depict botanical and horticultural subjects illustrated with hand-colored lithographs. Hill's work fell somewhere between art instruction and more technical scientific illustration, providing lessons in technique while emphasizing the need for accuracy in drawing and coloring in botanical illustration. The plates were printed by the workshop of James T. Bowen.

65

REPORT OF THE COMMITTEE APPOINTED BY THE PHILOMATHEAN SOCIETY OF THE UNIVERSITY OF PENNSYLVANIA TO TRANSLATE THE INSCRIPTION ON THE ROSETTA STONE

Philadelphia, 1859

In 1856 Thomas Conrad presented to the Philomathean Society of the University of Pennsylvania a facsimile in plaster of the famous Rosetta Stone. When the committee created to translate the inscriptions reported to the Society, they were asked to prepare a limited edition of their work. Facing the challenge of reproducing scripts for which no type existed, an undergraduate who had helped translate the text, Henry Morton, made over 400 lithographic stones which were printed by L. N. Rosenthal on Chesnut Street. The first edition, published in 1858, was quickly exhausted, and a second edition requested. As most of the stones for the first edition had been reground and used for multiple pages, the second edition of 1859 included new designs and different line endings. The Mellon copy is one of a handful of copies of the second edition printed on extra large paper.

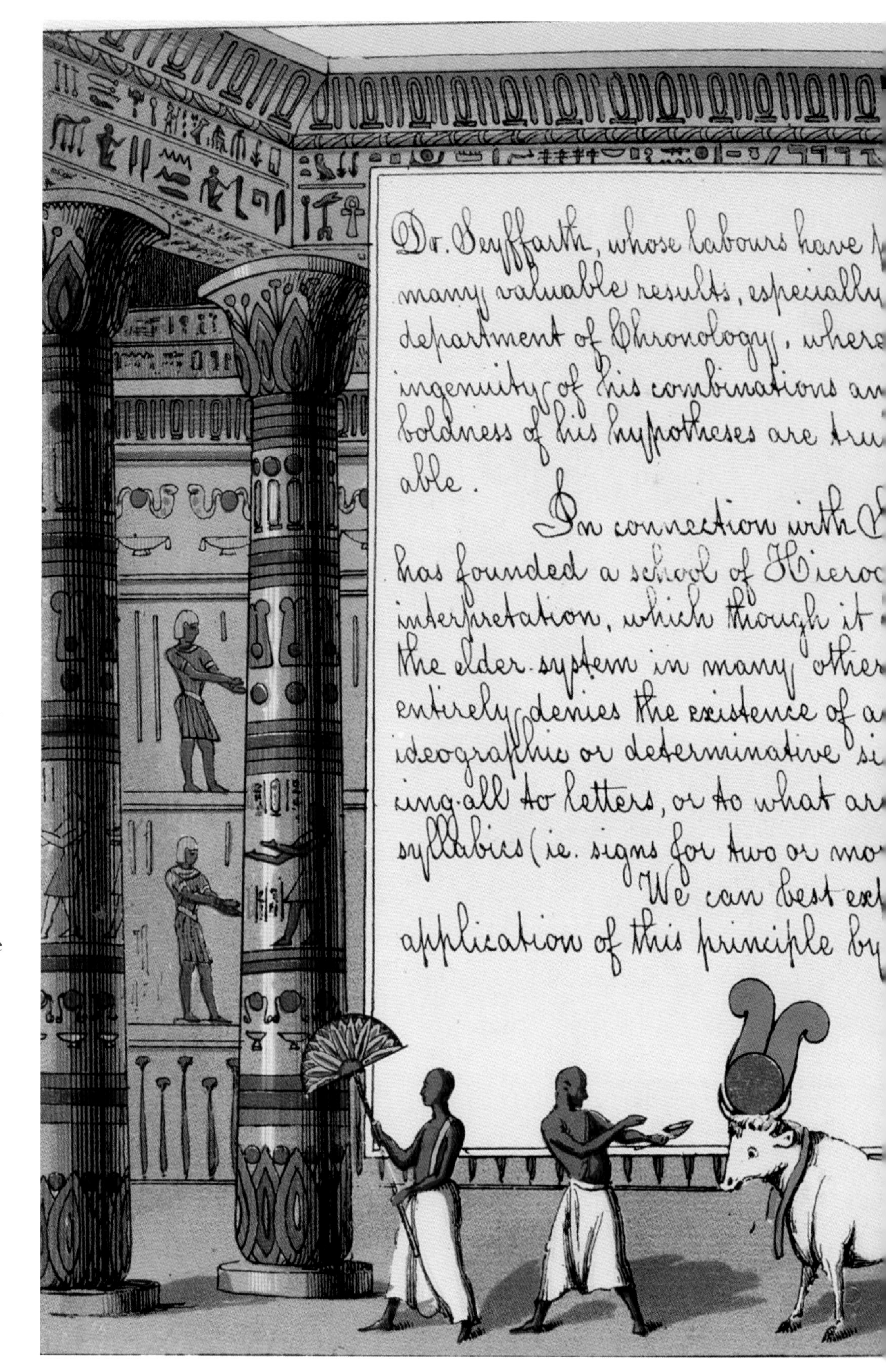

Dr. Seyffarth, whose labours have
many valuable results, especially
department of Chronology, where
ingenuity of his combinations an
boldness of his hypotheses are tru
able.
In connection with
has founded a school of Hiero
interpretation, which though it
the elder system in many other
entirely denies the existence of a
ideographic or determinative si
ing all to letters, or to what ar
syllabics (ie. signs for two or mo
We can best ex
application of this principle by

65. Illustrated border. Hand-colored lithograph.

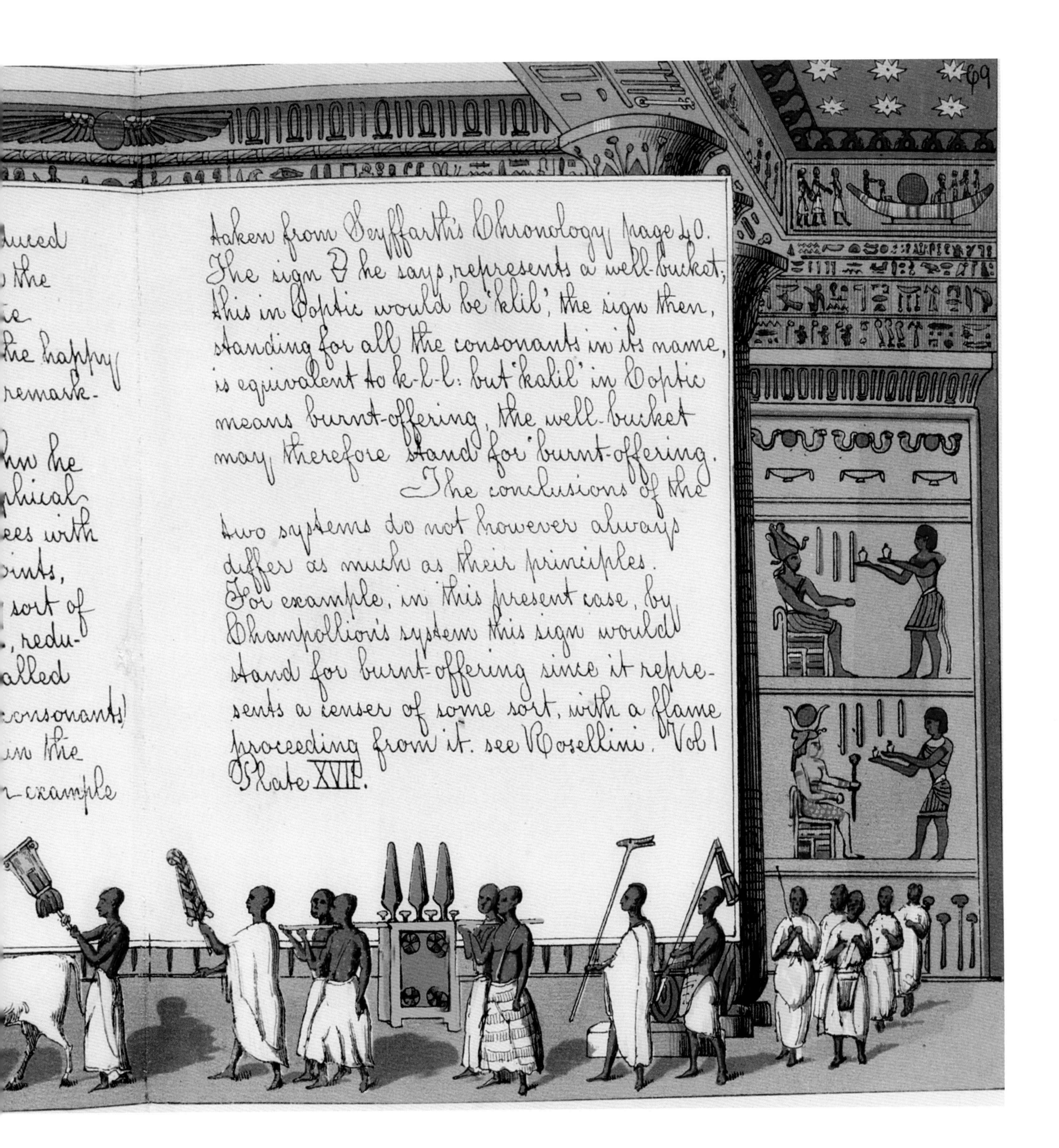

69

uced
the
e
the happy
remark-

hw he
phical
ees with
oints,
sort of
, redu-
alled
consonants)
in the
-example

taken from Seyffarth's Chronology page 40.
The sign ☐ he says, represents a well-bucket;
this in Coptic would be 'klil', the sign then,
standing for all the consonants in its name,
is equivalent to k-l-l: but 'kalil' in Coptic
means burnt-offering, the well-bucket
may therefore stand for 'burnt-offering.
The conclusions of the
two systems do not however always
differ as much as their principles.
For example, in this present case, by
Champollion's system this sign would
stand for burnt-offering since it represents a censer of some sort, with a flame
proceeding from it. see Rosellini. Vol 1
Plate XVII.

66

Louis Prang & Company

PROGRESSIVE PROOF BOOK FOR THOMAS MORAN'S *ON THE LOOKOUT* & *COLORADO CLIFFS*

Boston, 1872

The most successful American color printer of the nineteenth century, Louis Prang emigrated to America in 1850. His partnership, Prang and Mayer, produced black and white lithographs of monuments, buildings, and towns. In 1860 Prang bought out Mayer and moved into color printing of trade cards and other advertising for the mass market. Prang visited Germany in 1864 to study new lithographic techniques. The next year he began to print chromolithographic reproductions of famous works of art, using a laborious process of repeated printings with multiple stones and shades of colored ink to achieve more subtle and deeper colors. While his prints were expensive, post-Civil War affluence helped support an audience for them. Prang began copying the work of Old Masters but soon found he had more success with images of pets and western scenery, which he commissioned for reproduction. By 1870, his steam-driven presses were turning out 5,000 chromos a day and his firm had branch offices in New York, Philadelphia, San Francisco, London, Berlin, and Melbourne. The progressive proof book shows how two prints moved through twenty-two impressions to their final states.

66. *On the Lookout.*
Chromolithograph
after 7 stones and colors.

66. *On the Lookout.*
Chromolithograph
after 22 stones and colors.

67. Untitled view of Zinfandel grapes.
Chromo-lithograph.

67
Hannah Millard
GRAPES AND GRAPE VINES OF CALIFORNIA. PUBLISHED UNDER THE AUSPICES OF THE CALIFORNIA STATE VINICULTURAL ASSOCIATION. OLEOGRAPHED BY WM. HARRING FROM ORIGINAL WATER COLOR DRAWINGS BY MISS HANNAH MILLARD

San Francisco, 1877

The California wine industry had its first great flowering in the years after the Civil War. This beautiful and exceedingly rare book, with its chomolithographed plates of California wine grapes, was published by the innovative San Francisco printer Edward Bosqui. It exemplifies the mixture of artistry and technical detail found in the great illustrated natural history books of the nineteenth century. The bibliographer Robert Cowan suggested that the book was rare because "many copies were broken up to decorate the walls of numerous fine old saloons in San Francisco and elsewhere." This was probably the form in which most viewers experienced the plates, because few copies of the book have survived intact.

68. Open mouthed sleepers. Pencil drawing.

68
George Catlin
THE BREATH OF LIFE OR MAL-RESPIRATION

London, 1862.
With twenty-three original pencil drawings

Later re-issued as *Shut Your Mouth and Save Your Life*, this most peculiar of George Catlin's publications argued that Europeans and their American descendants would live healthier, happier lives if they adopted what he believed to be the Native American practice of breathing only through their noses. Catlin illustrated his point with pictures of squalling white infants compared with beaming, close-mouthed, Indian children. The Mellon copy of the first edition includes Catlin's original sketches.

69. *Catlin the Celebrated Indian Traveler and Artist.* Hand-colored lithograph.

69

George Catlin

COLT REVOLVER AND RIFLE SERIES

Chester, 1855

In July 1852 the United States Senate rejected a bill proposing the purchase of George Catlin's "Indian Gallery." The decision left Catlin bankrupt and cost him virtually all of the paintings and drawings he had exhibited in his various galleries. He sought patrons who would underwrite a trip to South America, where he planned to create a new series of paintings. Among the sponsors was Samuel Colt of Hartford, who had just begun to market his new revolver. Colt hired Catlin to make twelve pictures showing the artist using Colt's guns during his travels in South America and the West. Six of the paintings were turned into lithographs, but few sets seem to have been made. The scarcest of all Catlin prints, the Mellon set is one of four known.

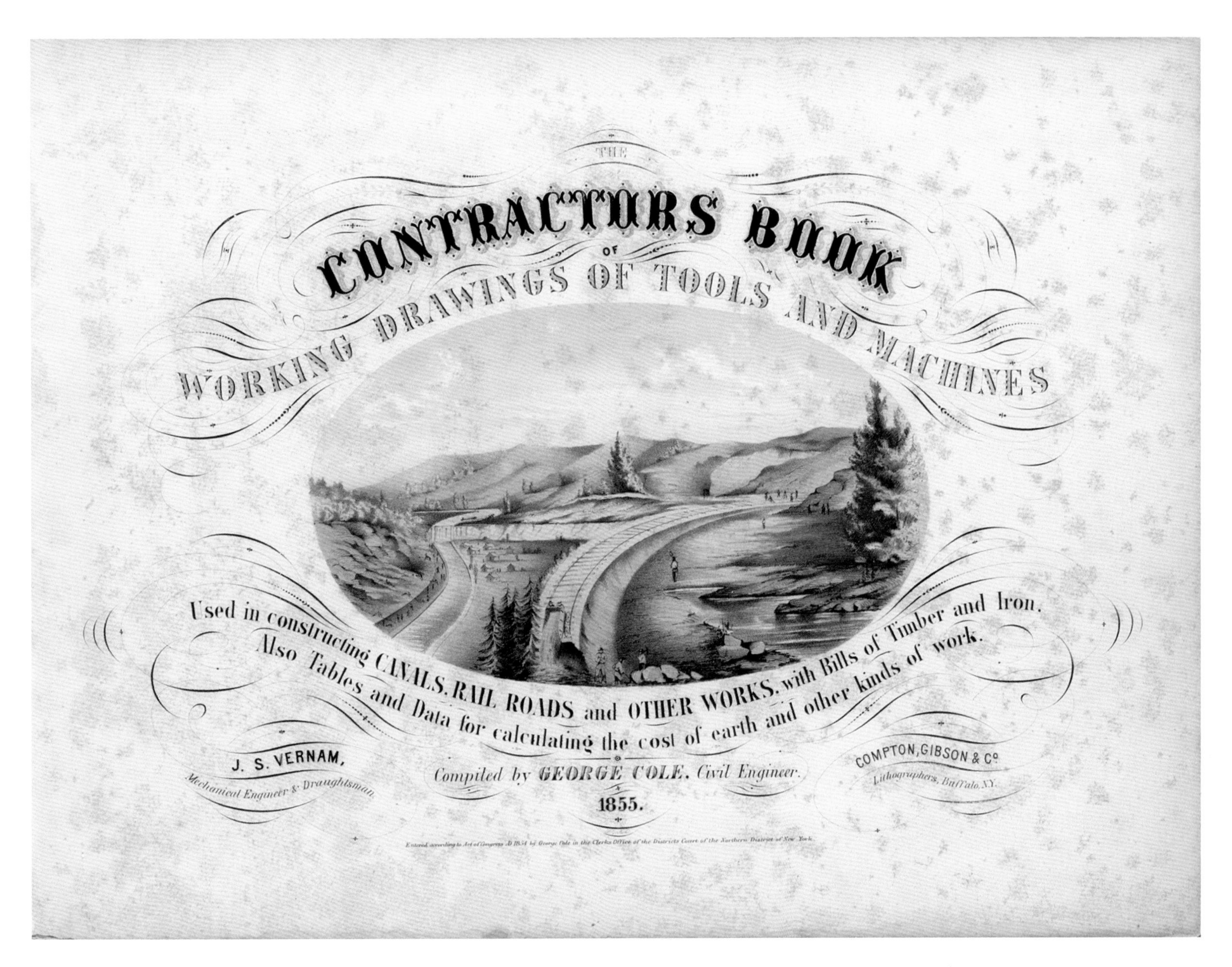
THE
CONTRACTORS BOOK
OF
WORKING DRAWINGS OF TOOLS AND MACHINES
Used in constructing CANALS, RAIL ROADS and OTHER WORKS, with Bills of Timber and Iron.
Also Tables and Data for calculating the cost of earth and other kinds of work.
J. S. VERNAM,
Mechanical Engineer & Draughtsman.
Compiled by GEORGE COLE, Civil Engineer.
1855.
COMPTON, GIBSON & Co.
Lithographers, Buffalo, N.Y.

70. Illustrated title page. Hand-colored lithograph.

70

George Cole

THE CONTRACTORS BOOK OF WORKING DRAWINGS OF TOOLS AND MACHINES

Buffalo, 1855

In the days before blueprint machines became common, lithography was an effective means of describing machine tools, far more concise and precise than words. Cole's catalog of tools used for constructing "canals, rail roads and other works" included estimated costs for performing various major construction projects, but its chief attraction must have been its large, elegantly executed illustrations.

71. Untitled drawing of a Hooker Company carriage. Ink drawing.

71. *Special Drawing* of a Hooker Company carriage. Ink drawing.

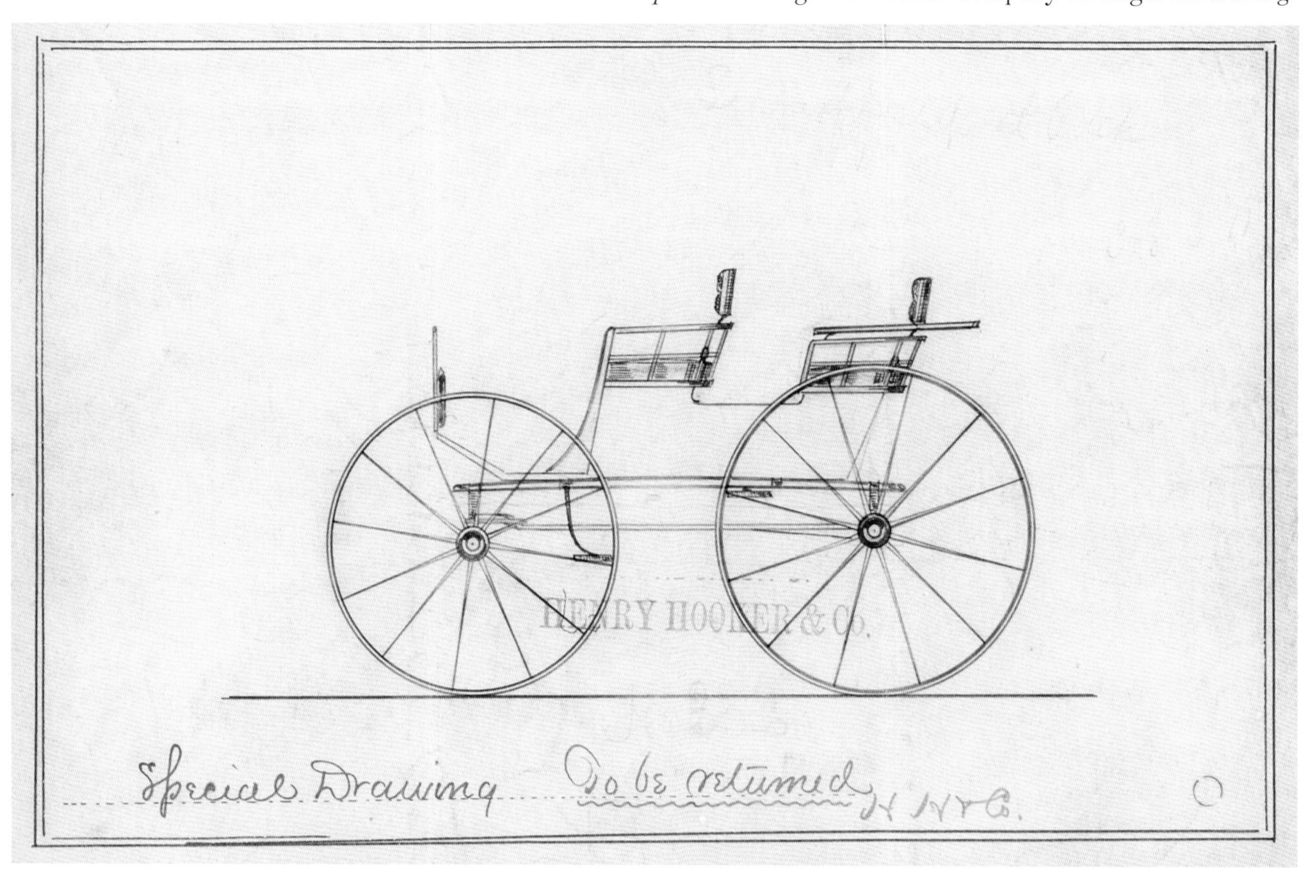

72. *Ingenio Acana.* Hand-colored lithograph.

71

Henry Hooker Company

ORIGINAL CARRIAGE DRAWINGS

New Haven, late nineteenth century

Henry Hooker & Company, incorporated in New Haven, Connecticut, in 1868, built light family and pleasure carriages for sale in the United States and foreign countries. Mellon's collection of twenty-four original drawings from the company's files show side views of phaetons, cabriolets, surreys, and concord carriages.

72

Justo G. Cantero

LOS INGENIOS COLECCION DE VISTAS DE LOS PRINCIPALES INGENIOS DE AZUCAR DE LA ISLA DE CUBA

Havana, 1857

Lithographic publications of nineteenth-century Havana reached their apogee with Cantero's lavish work depicting the sugar plantations of the island. Probably intended as a vanity publication for the wealthy owners of the principal estates, it was produced at a level of finish as fine as any European work of the period, thanks to the emigrant French lithographers who published it. Today, the bird's-eye views of the sugar works provide an unparalleled image of the material culture of an industry which did so much to shape the lives of people in the Caribbean, the American South, and other parts of the New World.

73. *Lieutenant, US Navy.* Hand-colored lithograph.

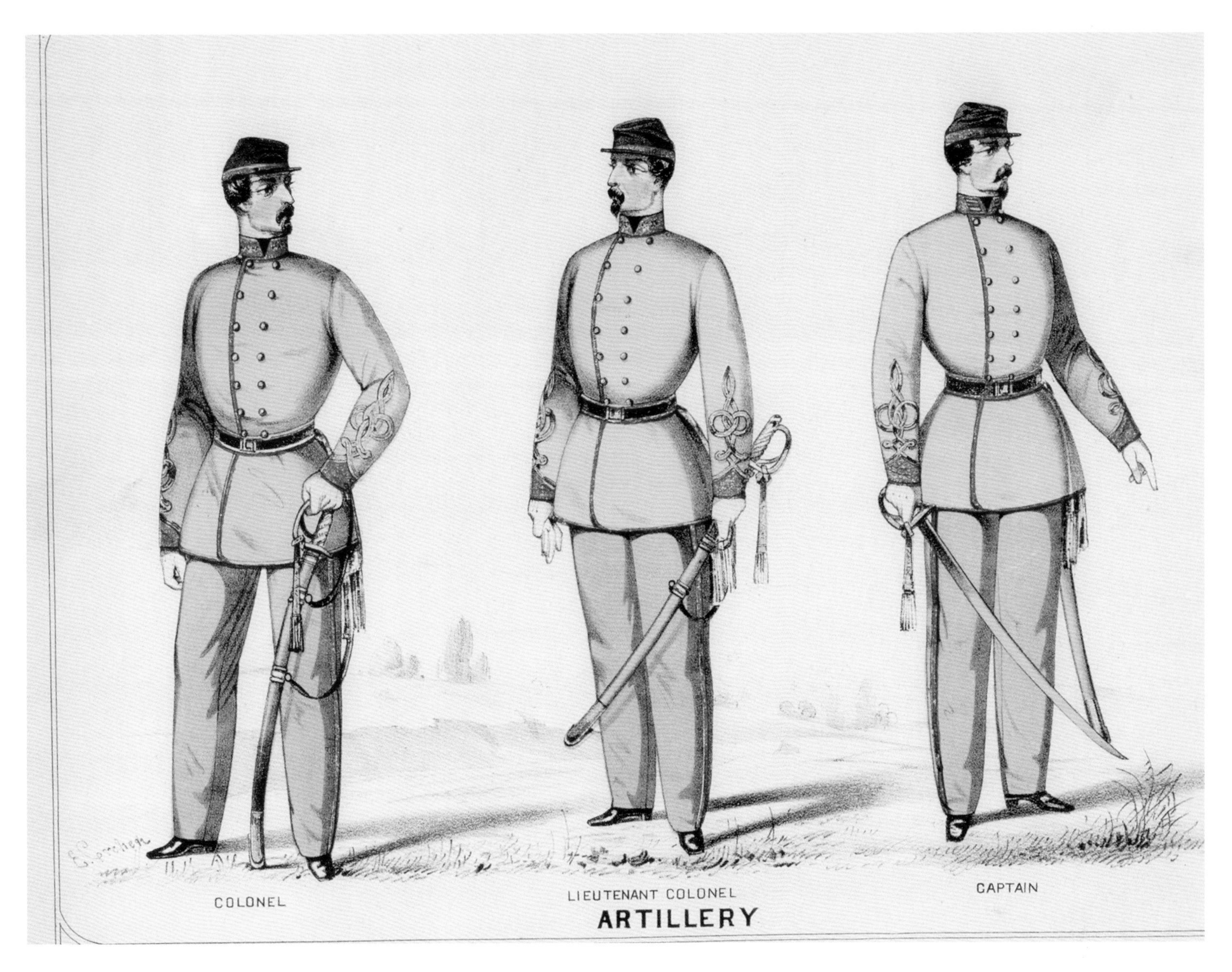

74. *Artillery.* Hand-colored lithograph.

73

William M. Huddy, editor

THE MILITARY MAGAZINE . . .

Philadelphia, 1839–June 1842

The Military Magazine was richly illustrated with hand-colored lithographs devoted either to military costume or to incidents from American military history. Depictions of uniforms showed the outfits of different ranks and services, sometimes worn by famous commanders. The historical scenes tend to be American victories, usually in the War of 1812. Issued serially as a magazine, this is one of the most elaborate American efforts in glorifying its army and navy, clearly modeled on the many British publications of the same genre.

74

UNIFORM AND DRESS OF THE ARMY OF THE CONFEDERATE STATES

Richmond, 1861

One of the few major illustrated works published in the Confederacy, this extravagant military costume book shows much fancier uniforms for the southern armies than later proved possible. Shortages of paper and supplies quickly curtailed the ability of the South to publish such books, which had in any case largely been printed in the North prior to the war.

75. *Chesnut Street.* Lithograph.

75

Julio H. Rae

RAE'S PHILADELPHIA PICTORIAL DIRECTORY & PANORAMIC ADVERTISER

Philadelphia, 1851

By 1850 virtually every major city in the United States supported the publication of an annual directory, an essential tool for rapidly expanding urban communities. In Philadelphia, the publisher Julio Rae created the first truly "visual directory" showing both sides of the main commercial thoroughfare of Chesnut Street, with storefronts illustrated side by side with advertising from the merchants. The concept was evidently too ambitious, because Rae did not produce any later editions, but it heralded a new era in display advertising.

76

Leon J. Fremaux

NEW ORLEANS CHARACTERS

New Orleans, 1876

Books illustrating typical trades and occupations, a common genre in European color plate books, are quite rare in American publications. This series of plates of New Orleans street vendors, hawkers, and pitchmen is the best example of its type printed in the United States. The plate shown here depicts an old auction house practice of having a doorman beat a drum on the sidewalk when a sale was about to commence inside.

76. *The Gemman that Beats the Drum for the Man that Sells.* Hand-colored lithograph.

Arts and Amusements

The Mellon bequest is extraordinarily rich in early American art manuals. Small publications, meant to be used rather than saved, these guides by British and American artists described how to make fine portraits, employ perspective, and use color to paint beautiful landscapes. Published in many different cities along the East Coast, they reflect the emergence of regional artistic communities during America's early national period and document the close relationship between original artists and the printing industry. As is the case with most "how to" manuals, few copies were collected and saved by institutions. Many of the works in the Mellon collection survive in fewer than a half dozen known copies.

The bequest also contains a wide variety of illustrations meant to amuse and entertain rather than instruct. The earliest extensively illustrated work of literature printed in the United States was a pirated copy of William Combe's *The Tour of Doctor Syntax, In Search of the Picturesque,* published in Philadelphia about 1819. Within a few decades, children's literature, gift books, Sunday school texts, comic books, sheet music, and political satire all relied upon images to enhance or carry their message. After the Civil War, American printers like McLoughlin Brothers of New York moved beyond books and reproductions of fine art to bring illustrative life to cards, board games, building blocks, and folding panoramas. One of the most successful and long-lived firms, the McLoughlin imprint ran from 1828 through 1978. Mellon collected a wide range of their products, many of which are shown here.

77. Untitled watercolor from Robertson's notebook.

77

Archibald Robertson

ELEMENTS OF THE GRAPHIC ARTS *and* MANUSCRIPT NOTEBOOK FOR AN UNPUBLISHED SEQUEL

New York, 1801–1802

This is the first work of art instruction published in the United States, accompanied by the manuscript for a second volume that was never issued. The author was a successful Scottish portrait painter who came to the United States at the invitation of Columbia College in 1791. He opened the Columbian Academy of Painting the following year, joined by his brother Alexander. The Robertsons were an important influence on the development of art in early New York, and the unpublished manuscript volume is a significant unexplored piece of evidence on their careers.

78. Untitled portrait with grid. Engraving.

78

Henry Williams

ELEMENTS OF DRAWING EXEMPLIFIED IN A VARIETY OF FIGURES AND SKETCHES OF PARTS OF THE HUMAN FORM . . .

Boston, 1814

Williams was both a portrait painter and engraver. His drawing instruction book is the most important to be issued after Robertson's work, giving the user basic lessons on how to draw, with a brief introduction and series of engraved plates. Unlike Lucas, who devoted himself to landscape, Williams focused almost entirely on portraiture and the human figure. He also pioneered a popular small, inexpensive format.

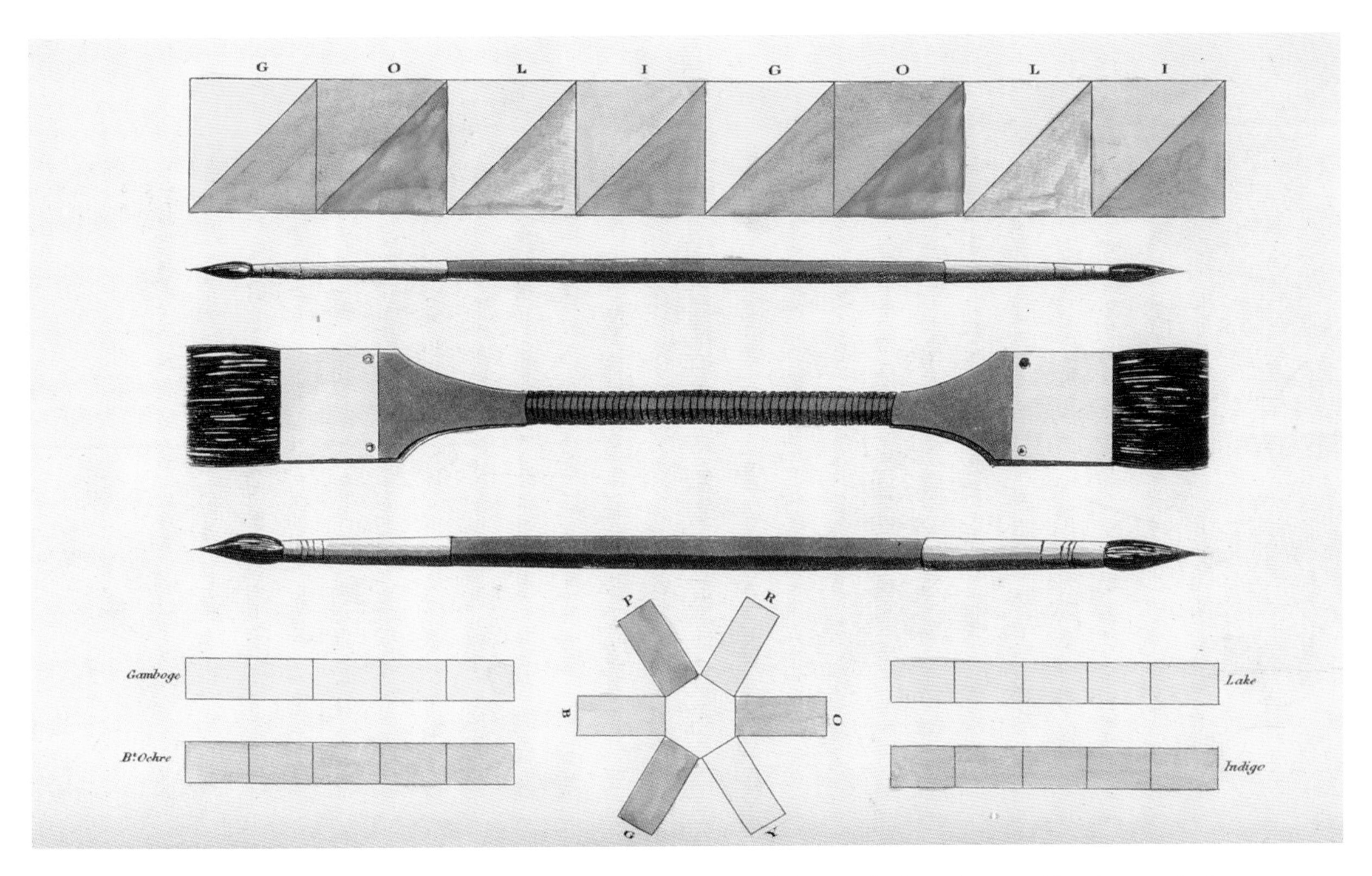

79. Untitled plate of color palettes and brushes. Hand-colored engraving.

79
Fielding Lucas

THE ART OF DRAWING, COLOURING AND PAINTING LANDSCAPES, IN WATER COLOURS

Baltimore, 1815

Lucas was a Baltimore publisher, one of the first to build a wide book distribution network throughout the United States. He also pioneered the use of color in American book illustration, especially in atlases and the two innovative art instruction works he wrote and published. This is the earlier and more modest of the two; the Beinecke already owned a copy of *Lucas's Progressive Drawing Book* (Baltimore, 1827). Both books used both uncolored and colored aquatints to demonstrate techniques in drawing and watercolor.

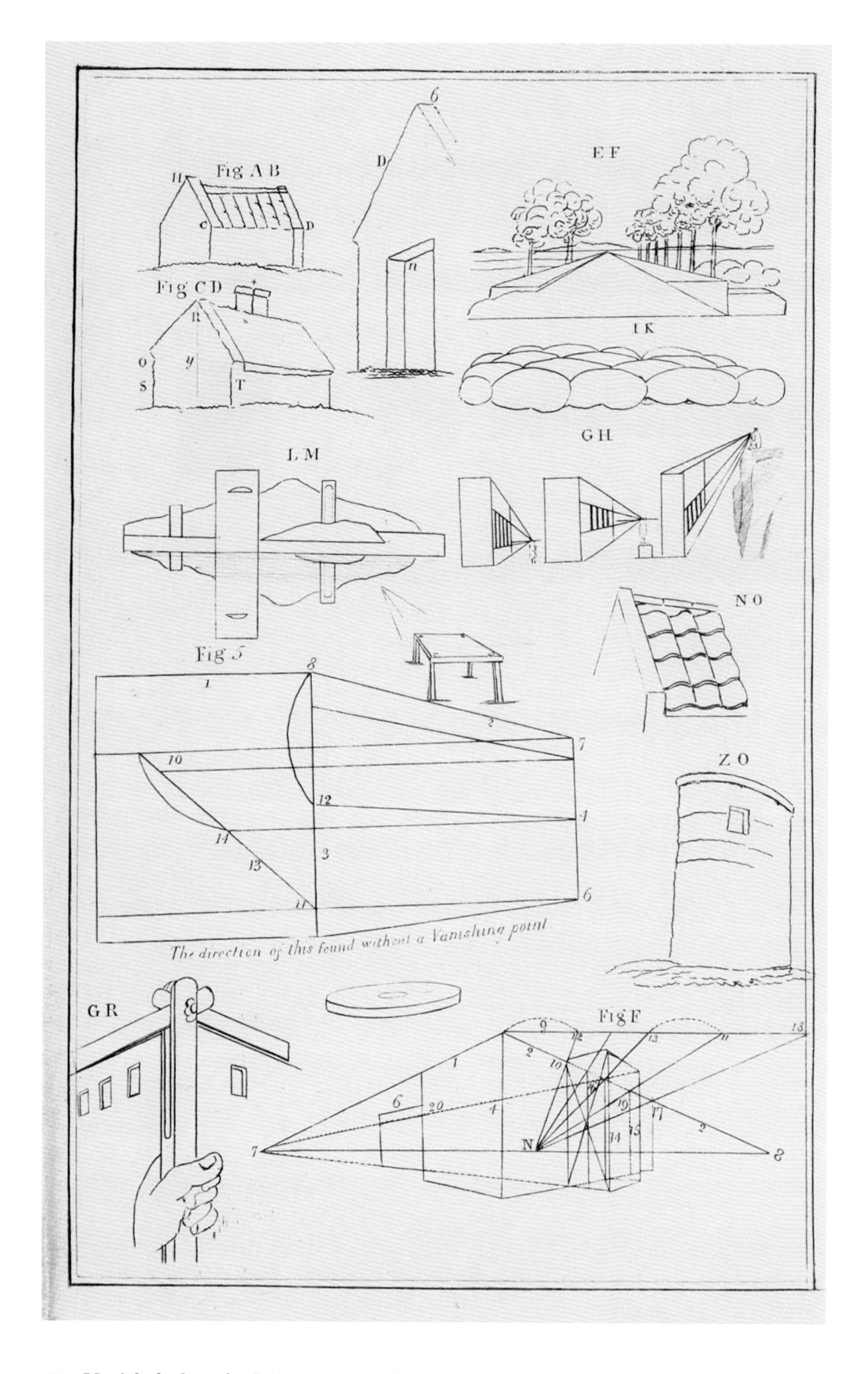

80. Untitled plate depicting perspective. Engraving.

80
John Varley
A PRACTICAL TREATISE ON PERSPECTIVE . . .

Baltimore, ca. 1820

Numerous English works on drawing were also republished in the United States. Varley's pamphlet, first published in London in 1815, was reprinted by Fielding Lucas. This was only the second work devoted to perspective issued in the United States.

81. *N 12* (Untitled view of an inn). Lithograph.

81

John T. Bowen

THE UNITED STATES DRAWING BOOK . . .

Philadelphia, 1839

Bowen issued this work just as his lithographic firm was becoming the most important in the nation. Over the next decade his shop produced the plates for the octavo edition of Audubon's *The Birds of America*, the large folio Audubon *Quadrupeds*, and most of the plates for McKenney and Hall's *History of the Indian Tribes*. Bowen's book of drawing instruction combined directions for work in pencil, chalk, crayon, and watercolor with views of rural and urban landmarks from the Natural Bridge in Virginia to Harvard University.

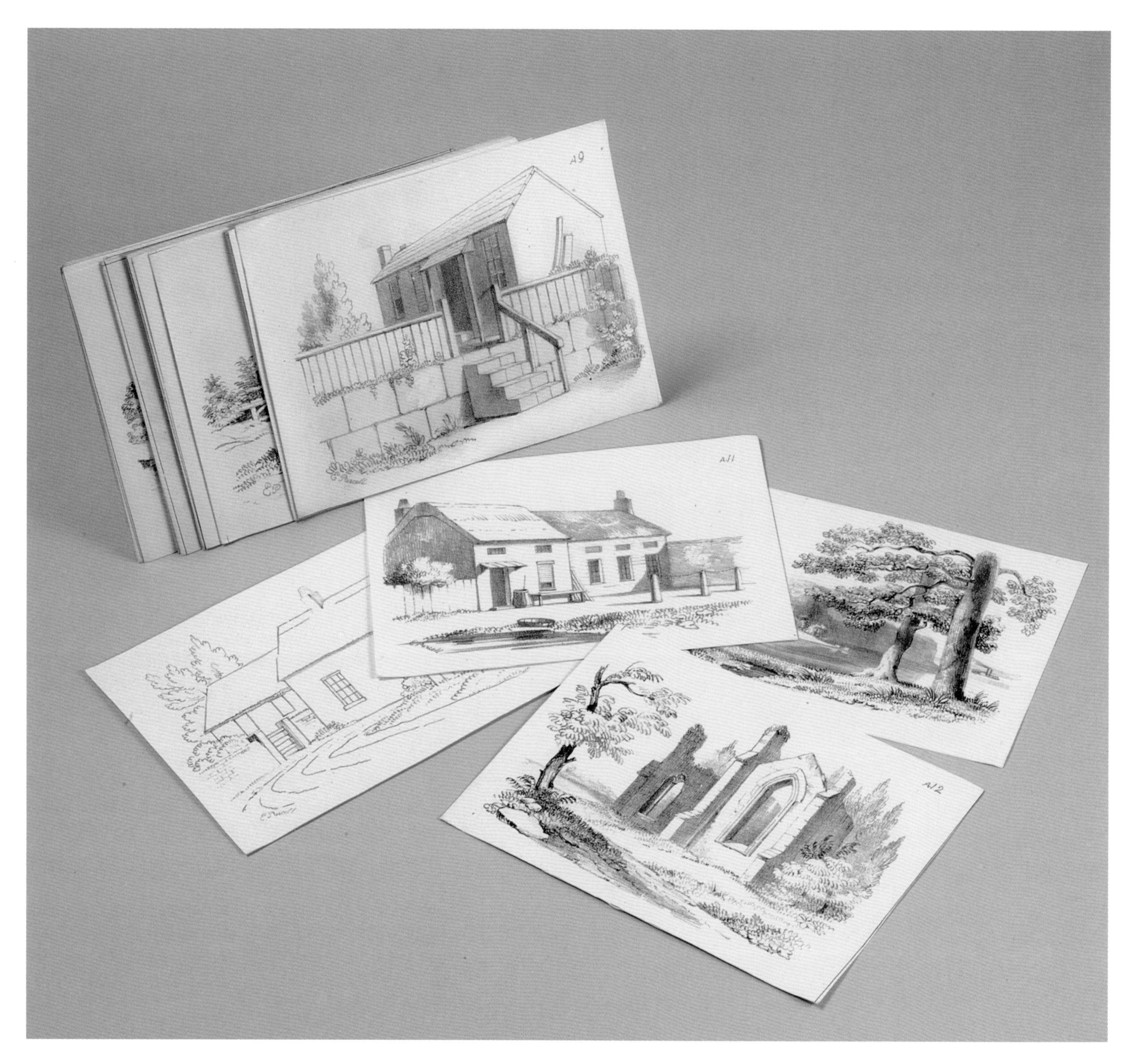

82. Instruction cards. Lithographs.

82

Edward Purcell

THIRD SERIES OF THE NEW YORK ARTISTS CLASS MANUAL OR LANDSCAPE LESSONS N. 3

New York, ca. 1840

Purcell was another artist of varied talents who seems to have made a living by wood engraving, genre paintings, and teaching drawing classes. He issued six sets of lessons lithographed on individual cards, each series slipcased in a paper sleeve.

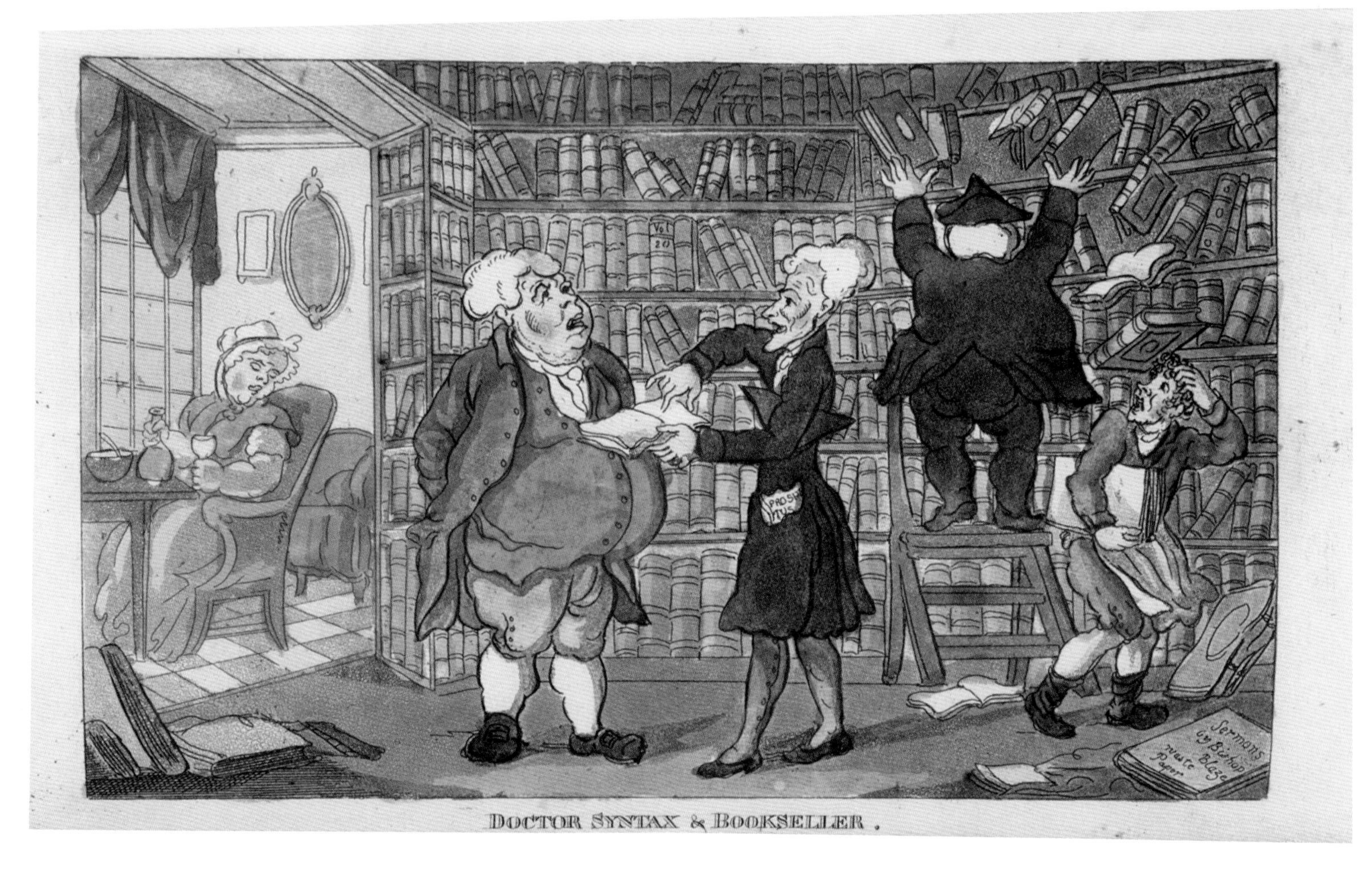

83. Doctor Syntax & Bookseller. Hand-colored aquatint.

83

William Combe

THE TOUR OF DOCTOR SYNTAX, IN SEARCH OF THE PICTURESQUE

Philadelphia, ca. 1819

This pirated American edition of William Combe's popular poem was the first extensively illustrated work of literature to be printed in the United States. The publisher and aquatint engraver William Charles, a British emigrant, did a passable job of imitating the original plates after Thomas Rowlandson. The book was sufficiently successful that the *Second Tour of Dr. Syntax* was pirated by the firm of Carey & Lea in 1822. The bulk of American literary publications in this era were reprints of European works, but this is a rare instance of an illustrated work being reprinted.

84. Untitled portrait. Chromolithograph.

84

Elizabeth Fries Ellet

THE CHARM: A SERIES OF ELEGANT COLORED GROUPS

Philadelphia, 1848

Gift books and annuals became a popular genre in the 1840s. Such volumes combined short fiction (generally sentimental), poetry, and brief essays with engravings or lithographs, usually in elaborately stamped cloth bindings. Monuments of early Victorian taste, they came suited to every pocketbook, from modest volumes cobbled together with discarded overrun plates to elaborate examples containing illustrations at the forefront of color printing technology. *The Charm* is among the most beautiful at the high end of the scale, with superbly executed chromolithographs of young women in faux-Gothic settings.

85

Anna Maria Hall

SKETCHES OF IRISH CHARACTER

Nashville, 1858

Color plates for nineteenth-century American books were often provided by printers other than those who created the text. Most frequently plates were imported from Europe to the large publishing centers of New York and Philadelphia. In this case, a collection of sentimental short stories about Irish life printed in Tennessee was illustrated with color plates engraved in Philadelphia. The addition of color brought a tinge of luxury to the book, appealing to a growing middle class readership.

85. *Mary Ryan's Daughter.* Chromolithograph.

86. *Kansas Pacific Grand March.* Lithograph.

86

Geo. Schleiffarth
KANSAS PACIFIC GRAND MARCH
St. Louis, 1872

By the middle of the nineteenth century, the illustration of sheet music cover pages had become a reliable source of business for lithographers throughout the country. Whether documentary or imaginative, the covers are a remarkable source of public imagery concerning such diverse topics as the Mexican War, the California Gold Rush, the building of railroads, the celebration of holidays, and the conduct of romance. The Mellon collection included a wide variety of songs and topics.

87

George Catlin

SALLE DU JARDIN BOTANIQUE, RUE ROYAL, BRUXELLES. COLLECTION DES TABLEAUX INDIENS DE G. CATLIN . . .

Brussels, ca. 1865

In the early 1860s, following his financial ruin and trips to South America, George Catlin retreated to Belgium, where he wrote several books about the federal government's Indian policy and set to work creating a new version of his Indian gallery. By mid-decade he was ready to resume exhibiting his work. This undated and previously unrecorded broadside announces a show of 550 oil paintings representing the Indians of the prairies, pampas, Rocky Mountains, and the Andes in which over 20,000 figures could be seen engaged in dances, games, religious ceremonies, or hunting activities.

Salle du Jardin Botanique,

RUE ROYALE, BRUXELLES.

COLLECTION DES TABLEAUX INDIENS

DE G. CATLIN,

visible depuis lundi, de 9 à 5 heures.

SAUVAGES DES AMÉRIQUES.

Cette Collection se compose de **550** tableaux à l'huile, contenant plus de **20,000** figures d'Indiens dans leurs **danses**, leurs **jeux**, leurs **cérémonies religieuses**, leurs **chasses**, etc., etc. Ces différentes scènes se passent dans les **PRAIRIES**, les **PAMPAS**, les **MONTAGNES ROCHEUSES** et les **ANDES**.

« Le MUSÉE INDIEN de CATLIN est une des collections les plus curieuses qu'on ait vues à Paris, tant à cause du caractère naïf de la peinture, qu'à cause de l'originalité des sujets qu'elle représente.

« M. Catlin a donc rapporté de son voyage aux Montagnes Rocheuses six cents toiles, portraits ou paysages, tous peints d'après nature. Parmi ces portraits, il y a des figures d'une beauté, d'une élégance superbes. Il y a des profils, le croirait-on, qui rappellent le type grec ou l'Antinoüs. Bien plus, dans les scènes de danse ou de combat, dans les fêtes ou les assemblées de tribus, on remarque très-souvent des personnages dont la pose, l'attitude, le geste ressemblent tout-à-fait à l'antique. Cela n'est pas, d'ailleurs, si surprenant pour qui veut réfléchir au caractère de la beauté antique. Qu'est-ce dont qui distingue l'art grec entre tous les arts? N'est ce pas la simplicité et le naturel? Les artistes grecs avaient le bonheur de trouver d'abord autour d'eux toutes les conditions premières de race, de climat, de civilisation, qui favorisent le développement de la beauté; et secondement, ils laissaient faire la nature et ne torturaient jamais le mouvement de leur modèle. Les hommes rapprochés de la nature ne se tortillent pas comme les civilisés. Le calme est d'ordre naturel, et c'est là un des premiers éléments de la beauté antique qu'on retrouve dans la *beauté sauvage*.

« Les paysagistes pourraient bien aussi étudier avec profit la peinture facile et vraie de M. Catlin qui n'est pourtant initié à aucun des procédés scabreux de l'art civilisé. M. Catlin peint tranquillement du premier coup, en mettant un ton juste et franc à côté d'un autre, et il ne paraît pas qu'il revienne jamais ni par glacis, ni par empâtement. Mais son sentiment est si vif et en quelque sorte si sincère, son exécution si naïve et si spontanée, que l'effet, vu juste, est rendu juste. Il a fait ainsi des ciels d'une transparence et d'une lumière bien difficile à obtenir, même pour les praticiens les plus habiles, des lointains d'une finesse rare et bien balancés entre la terre et le ciel. En présence de cette nature toute nouvelle, de ces formes singulières du pays, de cette couleur du ciel et des arbres, si originale, un peintre de profession se serait bien tourmenté pour exprimer toutes ces belles choses, et il y aurait sans doute mis beaucoup trop de ses préjugés et de sa personnalité civilisée. Il est très-heureux que M. Catlin ait été assez peintre pour faire tout bonnement sur la toile ce qu'il voyait, sans parti pris d'avance et sans convention européenne. Nous avons ainsi des steppes dont nous ne nous faisons pas une image, des buffles prodigieux, des chasses fantastiques et une foule d'aspects et de scènes plus intéressantes l'une que l'autre. Ici, c'est un marais vert tendre, entouré d'arbres sveltes et légers. Là, c'est la plaine infinie avec ses grandes herbes mouvantes comme les vagues d'une mer sans repos, et l'on aperçoit une course diabolique de quelques animaux dont on a peine à distinguer la forme et qui fendent l'immensité. C'est un buffle poursuivi par un cavalier penché sur la crinière de son cheval sauvage; mais au-dessus des herbes profondes, on ne voit que les épaules bossues du buffle et les oreilles dressées du cheval. Quel drame! Où vont-ils? où s'arrêteront-ils? Quelques autres tableaux présentent les aventures de la navigation et de la guerre, des chasses où les hommes, couverts de peaux de loup, s'avancent à quatre pattes pour surprendre les buffles, où les chevaux sauvages sont enveloppés de lacets perfides, des cérémonies religieuses où de volontaires martyrs se font pendre et torturer en l'honneur du Grand Esprit. » (Extrait du « *Constitutionnel.* »)

PRIX D'ENTRÉE : 50 centimes. — Enfants, 25 centimes.

Bruxelles. — Imp. de C. Coomans, rue Allard, 20.

87. *Salle du Jardin Botanique.* Letterpress.

88. Hand-colored panorama, mounted on rollers in a wooden box.

88

EXCURSION VIEWS OF NARRAGANSETT BAY AND BLOCK ISLAND

The Abbey Collection, which Mellon purchased *en bloc* and ultimately gave to the Yale Center for British Art, contained both grand color plate books and smaller entertainments such as panoramas, peep shows, and games. Mellon continued to add to the Abbey books and objects throughout his collecting career. This panorama, contained within a wooden box and worked by small cranks, shows the view from a steamship sailing down Narragansett Bay from Providence, Rhode Island, and out to Block Island.

89

Toby Thistle (pseud.)

DEATH OF COMMON SENSE . . .

1809

Featuring such roles as the King of Bedlammania, the Prince of Whales, the Duke of North Street, and Sir Arthur O. Critic among others, the *Death of Common Sense* is a three-act political satire set in England, but evidently created in the United States. The present manuscript copy of the play appears to have belonged to a Mr. Mercer, who is listed as playing the role of Mr. Critic in performance at the Royale Theater. Dated on the cover "Baltimore May 12, 1809," the manuscript includes five watercolors by Gabriel Gamboge.

89. *The Prince of Whales.* Pen, ink, and watercolor drawing.

90. *Death and the Devil laying a snare . . . .* Lithograph.

90. *The Overland Party . . . Captured by Sap-Head Indians.* Lithograph.

90
S. F. Baker
OUTLINE HISTORY OF AN EXPEDITION TO CALIFORNIA

New York, 1849

In the eighteenth century, British artist William Hogarth transformed the anonymous broadsheet picture story. With an unrivalled sense of satire he added topical reference and social insight in prints that examined the pretensions of all classes of society. Early in the nineteenth century, Rodolphe Töpffer, a Geneva schoolmaster, further developed the narrative aspect of caricature and cartooning by creating oblong story books of as many as 100 pages in which his absurd antiheroes struggled desperately, comically, but fruitlessly against fate, nature, and irrational society. By the 1840s, similar "comic books" began to appear in both Britain and United States. Gold fever was a popular target for the cartoonists and Baker's *Outline History* is one of several works that lampooned the '49ers and their quest for quick and easy wealth.

91. A Mormon and his wives dancing to the devil's tune. Hand-colored lithograph.

91
Increase and Maria Van Deusen

STARTLING DISCLOSURES OF THE WONDERFUL CEREMONIES OF THE MORMON SPIRITUAL-WIFE SYSTEM

New York, 1850

The Van Deusens' polemic against Mormon polygamy was first published in Albany in 1847 under the title *Positively True: A dialogue between Adam and Eve, the Lord and the Devil: Called the endowment: As was acted by twelve or fifteen thousand, in secret, in the Nauvoo Temple.* The New York 1850 printing is generally considered to be the fifth edition of the work; at least ten editions were distributed before 1865. Effectively blending satire and doctrinal argument, the illustrations make clear the Van Deusens' belief that Mormonism was a diabolical device.

92. *He resigns his pretensions.* Lithograph.

He bears off the wooden spoon. Lithograph.

92

William T. Peters, Hugh Peters, & Garrick Mallery

THE COLLEGE EXPERIENCE OF ICHABOD ACADEMICUS

New Haven, 1849

An annotated copy found in the Yale University Archives identifies the authors and illustrator as Yale undergraduates and establishes the date of publication as 1849. Written "to please both Collegian and Graduate; the one by picturing his present pastimes, the other by freshening the treasured tints of memory," it joins a similar book from Harvard, *College Scenes*, as the earliest caricatures of American college life. In one of the panels reproduced here, Ichabod is awarded the wooden spoon, traditionally given to the member of the junior class with the lowest academic ranking. After graduating from Yale College in 1850, Garrick Mallery went on to become the nineteenth century's foremost scholar of American Indian sign language and picture writing.

93. *Cheek by Jowl.* Tinted lithograph.

93
Augustus Kollner
CITY SIGHTS FOR COUNTRY EYES
Philadelphia, ca. 1855

Augustus Kollner was the kind of multi-talented, market-sensitive, professional artist characteristic of many northeastern cities in the middle of the nineteenth century. Born in Düsseldorf in 1813, he trained in Frankfurt before emigrating to the United States. A lithographer, he was a prolific illustrator of children's and sporting books. He also appears to have traveled widely and worked as an itinerant artist. In the decade before the Civil War he prepared several titles for the American Sunday School Union of Philadelphia. The present work, consisting of twelve plates and twelve brief essays, was listed in the Union's catalogues from January 1857 through 1893. Each plate illustrates a moral message while depicting a scene from everyday life.

94. *The New Country Pioneers.* Hand-colored lithograph.

94
Augustus Kollner
THE NEW COUNTRY PIONEERS
Philadelphia, ca. 1855

This bound volume of twelve plates accompanied by brief essays has no title page; our title is drawn from the first print in the book. The plates, which trace the development of an unspecified, generic frontier community through the course of a year, identify Kollner as artist and supply the Sunday School Union as publisher. The composition resembles that of *City Sights for Country Eyes*, but it is unclear how many copies may have been printed.

95. Playing cards. Chromolithographs.

95
McLoughlin Brothers

GAME OF DR. FUSBY. M.D.A.S.S.

New York, ca. 1860

Paul Mellon's illustrated Americana included an eclectic assortment of books, games, and toys from the distinguished American publishing firm of McLoughlin Brothers. The firm traced its origins to John McLoughlin, a young Scottish immigrant who purchased a used hand press and produced his first children's pamphlet in 1828. Twenty-five years later, his two sons had taken over the firm. They introduced American children to British illustrators Randolph Caldecott, Kate Greenaway, and Walter Crane. When Civil War isolation contributed to the emergence of a truly American school of illustration, McLoughlin's premier artist became Thomas Nast, the well-known political cartoonist who created the most familiar image of Santa Claus. As the firm's children's book business thrived, they added toys, games, paper dolls, and other novelty items to their merchandise.

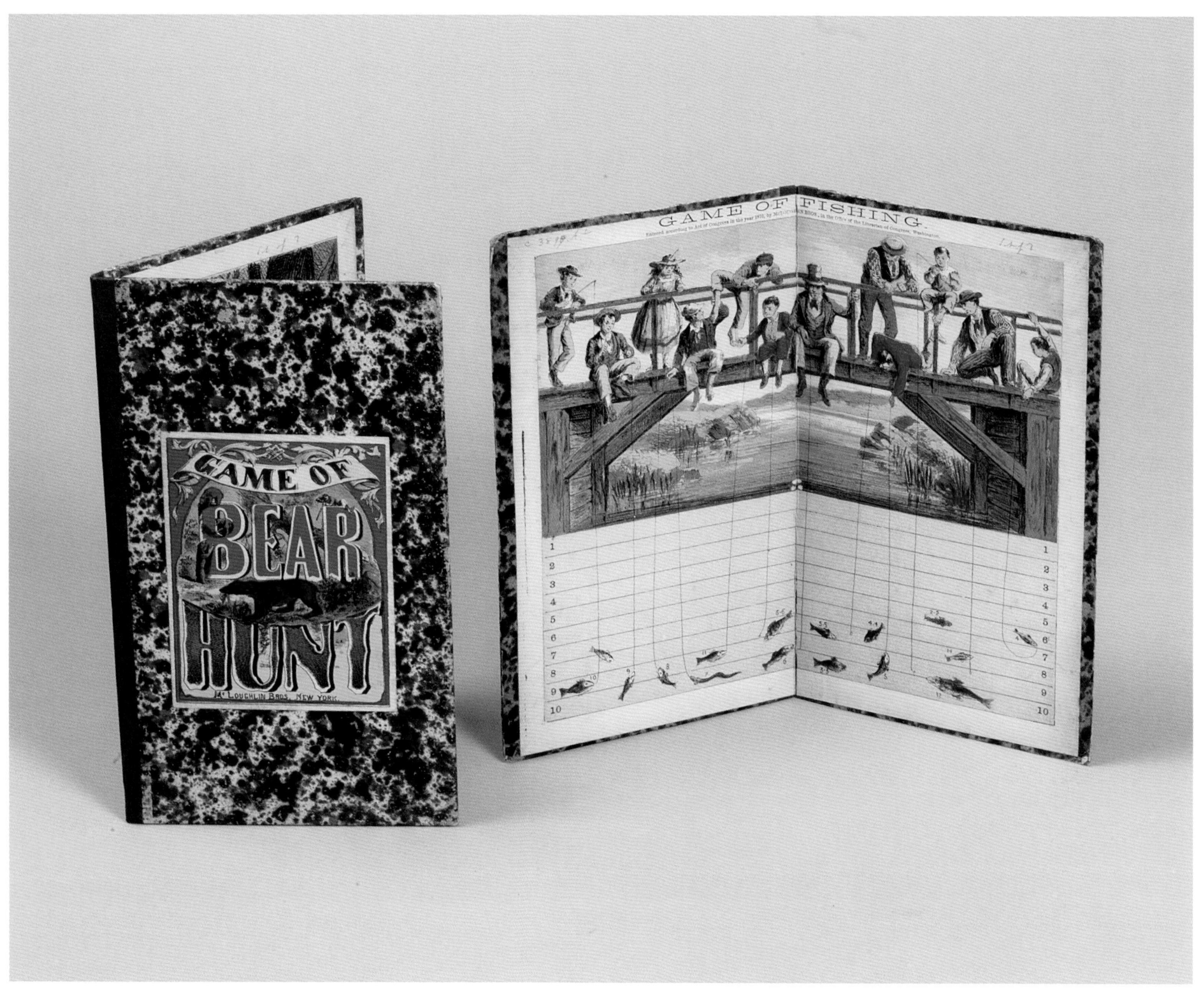

96. *Game of Bear Hunt* and *Game of Fishing*. Chromolithographs.

96

McLoughlin Brothers

FOLDING BOARD GAMES

New York, 1870

One of the country's leading color printers, McLoughlin Brothers eagerly adopted new technology. They progressed from hand-stenciling to wood engraving in color to chromolithography. They were the first American printers to use zinc plates. In 1870 they opened a new factory in Brooklyn, said to be the largest such establishment in the United States. A staff of seventy-five artists was employed to design books and board games. When John McLoughlin Jr. died in 1907, the obituary in *Publishers Weekly* observed, "Every child in the land knows the McLoughlin toys and books, and even across the seas their edition of Mother Goose has been sent printed in many languages. In fact, the history in the last decade of colored toy books for youngsters is the history of Mr. McLoughlin and his firm."

97. *The Brownie Blocks.* Chromolithographs mounted on blocks.

97
Palmer Cox
THE BROWNIE BLOCKS
New York, 1891

The Brownies, a race of elfin creatures who delighted in doing good works, were the creation of Palmer Cox, one of McLoughlin Brothers' most important authors. Born in Canada, Cox emigrated to San Francisco in 1863, where he worked as a ship's carpenter. After several California periodicals published his verse works, Cox moved to New York City, where he found his calling as an author of children's literature. Between 1880 and 1920 he wrote nearly 100 stories about the Brownies. Published first in *St. Nicholas Magazine,* many of the stories were turned into McLoughlin Brothers' books. The three-act play *Palmer Cox's Brownies* opened in 1895 and ran for nearly five years. Millions of young consumers and their parents bought Brownie toys and Brownie-adorned items that ranged from pencil boxes to clothing to wallpaper to these building blocks printed by McLoughlin Brothers. Regarded as a pioneer in writing nondidactic books for children, Cox is also considered a founder of the field of children's fantasy literature.

98. Pop-up scene. Chromolithograph.

98

BUFFALO BILL'S WILD WEST PANORAMA FOR CHILDREN

London, 1890

By 1890 the Indian Wars of the Great Plains had become the stuff of European as well as American popular culture. An authentic frontier scout and Indian fighter, Buffalo Bill Cody gained national fame as a dime-novel hero. He first appeared on stage in Chicago in 1872; in 1883 he staged his first open-air entertainment in Nebraska. In 1887 he took his show to London where it played during Queen Victoria's Jubilee. Two years later the show toured Europe, opening to large crowds in Paris. Pop-up children's books are only one example of the assorted merchandise that accompanied the "Wild West" craze.

Acknowledgments

First and foremost, we are deeply grateful to the late Paul Mellon for his legacy of books, the culmination of a lifetime of gifts to the Yale University Library. Mr. Mellon's concern for the Yale collections has immeasurably enhanced the materials available here for research.

We also owe a debt of gratitude to the executors of Mr. Mellon's estate. Beverly Carter and Frederick A. Terry Jr., operating under the terms of Mr. Mellon's will, were chiefly responsible for the distribution of the materials in this exhibition to the Beinecke Library and to the library at the Yale Center for British Art. All of the staff of the Brick House, Beverly Carter, Michelle Tompkins, Eugene Howard, Linda Cook, and Carolyn Colbert, aided in the transfer of books both to the Beinecke and on a much larger scale to the Center for British Art. Their careful help and attention to detail is deeply appreciated.

We have spent many hours studying Mr. Mellon's books with our colleague Elisabeth Fairman, Curator of Rare Books and Archives at the Yale Center for British Art. Her insight and advice have been essential in shaping this catalog and the exhibition it records. We also appreciate the generous assistance of Constance Clement, Acting Director of the Center, and Timothy Goodhue, the Center's registrar, in granting us permission to exhibit and reproduce items numbered 1, 25, 30, 35, 44, 45, 77, and 88 in this catalog.

Barbara Shailor, Director of the Beinecke Rare Book & Manuscript Library, has offered enthusiastic support for this project from our earliest conversations with her. Suzanne Rutter, Head of Technical Services at Beinecke Library, and her staff, especially Karin Marinuzzi and Amelia Prostano, have overseen the receipt and handling of the Mellon bequest. Their knowledge of the books and manuscripts in the bequest, as well as their friendly and timely assistance, made the preparation of the exhibition and catalog much easier than we expected. We thank Hanna Shell, Christa Sammons, and Susan Imhoff for graciously reviewing the manuscript. Susan also compiled the index for the catalog.

Finally, we salute our designer, Greer Allen, for the energy, imagination, and skill he brought to the project. He oversaw not only the layout and typography of the catalog but also played an essential role in supervising the production of the illustrations. We are honored to have collaborated with him in the making of this book.

Index *refers to entry numbers*

DESIGN

Greer Allen

COLOR SEPARATION

Professional Graphics, Inc., Rockford, Illinois

PRINTING & BINDING

CS Graphics Pte, Ltd., Singapore